The Holy Spirit is working  grandparents to impact their grandparent, you have a unique opportunity to bless and nurture faith in future generations. *Pass the Legacy* will encourage your heart, expand your vision, and give you practical ways to point the hearts of your grandkids to Jesus. I know you will be blessed through Catherine's journey, wisdom, and most importantly the Scriptures that she shares in this great book.

– **DR. ROB RIENOW**,
FOUNDER, VISIONARY FAMILY MINISTRIES

Maybe you sense it too. Why are the resources on Christian grandparenting so rare? So I love it when a grandparent lifts his or her voice to speak with wisdom and urgency into the near void. Catherine is a passionate advocate for a grandparent's role in a grandchild's spiritual journey. But through the clear call to intentional spiritual grandparenting, something else makes an appearance...the joy and beauty that is the unique relationship of a grandchild and grandparent walking with God together. Love shines through this writing. I predict: Catherine's writing will draw you closer to your grandkids as you share your spiritual journey together.

– **VALERIE BELL**, CEO AWANA

The book you hold in your hand was written by a grandmother who truly gets it when she tells you, "You can make a difference in your grandchild's life". Catherine Jacobs writes, not only at a practical level, but soul level. And in so doing, she reminds us that our effectiveness as grandparents starts with the conditions of our own souls. The Seven Keys Catherine has developed for passing a legacy that matters need to be learned and put into practice by every grandparent who claims to be a follower of Christ. *Pass the Legacy* is a practical, powerful tool for grandparents who take their biblical roles seriously.

Warning: If you don't take it seriously, don't read this book. Truth, conviction and transformation may lead to a changed heart.

– CAVIN HARPER, FOUNDER AND PRESIDENT,
CHRISTIAN GRANDPARENTING NETWORK

Many of us grandparents are having a difficult time understanding the culture in which our grandchildren are growing up today. Their world is much different than the one we grew up in or in which we raised our children. However, God has given us a call to reach the hearts and minds of our dear grandchildren and future generations to love and follow Jesus. The enemy wants to distract and steal our grandchildren and their parents from walking with the Lord. Catherine Jacobs gives you seven key principles that will equip you to significantly impact your grandchildren and their parents with a spiritual legacy.

– LILLIAN PENNER, CO-CHAIRMAN OF PRAYER FOR
CHRISTIAN GRANDPARENTING NETWORK,
AUTHOR OF *GRANDPARENTING WITH A PURPOSE*

Pass the Legacy is book that every grandparent will benefit from. Catherine writes with an eye on eternity and a grounding in God's Word. There are many books on grandparenting, but Catherine's is unique because she calls grandparents back to the essentials, to the things that matter and can transform your family. Catherine is a seasoned grandparenting guide who can show you the path to impacting your family for Christ. Do yourself a favor and pick up a copy today.

– DR. JOSH MULVIHILL, AUTHOR OF *BIBLICAL GRANDPARENTING*
AND EXECUTIVE DIRECTOR OF CHURCH
AND FAMILY MINISTRY AT RENEWANATION.

In this delightful book, Catherine Jacobs gives grandparents a helpful blueprint for leveraging the immense amount of love and influence we already have for our grandchildren. Read it and learn how you can leave a spiritual legacy that will last for many generations to come.

— **WAYNE RICE** - CO-FOUNDER OF YOUTH SPECIALTIES AND DIRECTOR OF CONFERENCING, LEGACY COALITION

Catherine Jacobs is a Champion for Grandparents. I believe this book will encourage and equip grandparents to take seriously the opportunities and influence that the Lord has given them to reach the hearts of their grandchildren and children with the love of Christ.

As I read through the pages, I can hear Catherine's passion. Thankfully, she gives us practical steps and engaging stories that will help grandparents take action as they revisit the Lord's call on their lives.

Catherine has been busy in the field speaking throughout South Carolina and our country. I am thankful for her obedience through the years. She introduced our Diocese to this vital ministry. As a result, we have seen many churches and people catch the biblical vision for being a Godly parent and grandparent.

I believe this book will be a great resource for ministry leaders, family ministries, parents and grandparents. Thank you, Catherine! May this book fuel revival and restoration of the family for God's Glory.

— **PETER ROTHERMEL**, COORDINATOR FOR THE DEPARTMENT OF CHRISTIAN FAITH FORMATION FOR THE DIOCESE OF SOUTH CAROLINA

Catherine Jacobs' book, *Pass the Legacy: 7 Keys for Grandparents Making a Difference,* is a mighty assignment from the Lord. It carries an anointing to lead the young and the old into an intimate relationship with their Lord and Savior. As I read the pages I could visualize so many grandparents having "aha moments" where they feel a wonderful sense of hope about their role of passing the legacy of faith to their grandchildren. Along with unwrapping this sense of hope will come an opportunity for grandparents, themselves, to draw even closer to the Lord.

– Nena Jackson, co-author of Fruit That Lasts

Having twenty one grandchildren of our own, we are always looking for help in how to be wise grandparents. Catherine Jacobs has given us a timely book that is relevant, practical, and encouraging; filled with ideas that are helpful and thoughtful. We recommend *Pass the Legacy* wholeheartedly.

– Dr. John Yates, the Rector of The Falls Church,
Falls Church, Virginia
– Susan Yates, author and speaker Christian women

Catherine Jacobs pours out her passion for the Lord and the role He ordained for grandparents in her first book, *Pass the Legacy*. She challenges her readers to defy cultures' lies about the golden years and accept the fact God calls them to pass their spiritual legacies to future generations. She arms her readers with practical advice found in her "7 Keys for Grandparents Making a Difference," which include praying fervently, healing broken relationships and leaving a written legacy of love. For Christian grandparents who haven't considered the importance of their roles in the lives of their grandchildren, *Pass the Legacy* is an insightful and enjoyable read.

– Sherry Schumann, co-director of the Prayer Ministry for
Christian Grandparenting Network, director of Prayer Ministry
for Legacy Coalition, author, speaker, published writer

PASS THE LEGACY

PASS THE LEGACY

7 Keys for Grandparents Making a Difference

Awakening a retired generation to reach a wandering
generation so together we can lead the youngest generation
to know, love, and serve the Lord Jesus Christ

Catherine Jacobs
"Nina"

ELM HILL

A Division of
HarperCollins Christian Publishing

www.elmhillbooks.com

PASS THE LEGACY
7 Keys for Grandparents Making a Difference

All rights reserved. No portion of this book may be reproduced, stored in a retrieval system, or transmitted in any form or by any means—electronic, mechanical, photocopy, recording, scanning, or other—except for brief quotations in critical reviews or articles, without the prior written permission of the publisher.

Published in Nashville, Tennessee, by Elm Hill, an imprint of Thomas Nelson. Elm Hill and Thomas Nelson are registered trademarks of HarperCollins Christian Publishing, Inc.

Elm Hill titles may be purchased in bulk for educational, business, fund-raising, or sales promotional use. For information, please e-mail SpecialMarkets@ ThomasNelson.com.

All Scripture quotations, unless otherwise indicated, are taken from the Holy Bible, New International Version˚, NIV˚. Copyright © 1973, 1978, 1984, 2011 by Biblica, Inc.˚ Used by permission of Zondervan. All rights reserved worldwide. www.Zondervan.com. The "NIV" and "New International Version" are trademarks registered in the United States Patent and Trademark Office by Biblica, Inc.˚

Scripture quotations marked KJV are from the King James Version. Public domain.

Scripture quotations marked NLT are from the Holy Bible, New Living Translation. © 1996, 2004, 2007, 2013, 2015 by Tyndale House Foundation. Used by permission of Tyndale House Publishers, Inc., Carol Stream, Illinois 60188. All rights reserved.

Library of Congress Cataloging-in-Publication Data

Library of Congress Control Number: 2018950366

ISBN 978-1-595558671 (Paperback)
ISBN 978-1-595558794 (Hardbound)
ISBN 978-1-595558688 (eBook)

DEDICATION

To my dear children and grandchildren, I first and foremost dedicate this book. Without your presence, your love and your encouragement, I would not have a book to write. It is through each of you that I have been shown by our Lord Jesus Christ the profound joy of being a parent and grandparent. Always remember how much I love you! More importantly, embrace the overflowing love of our Heavenly Father to you through His Son, Jesus. Never forget He is closer to you than your next breath. I cherish each moment I share with you on the face of this earth. I breathlessly wait for the day when we will stand *together* in our heavenly home forever.

To Cavin Harper, I also dedicate this book. You were the first one to see the potential given to me by the Lord to write a book. Thank you for seeing in me what I could not see in myself. Also, thank you for being miles ahead of me in this ministry. It has been an honor to follow your lead.

To Peter Rothermel, I dedicate this book. You were always present to boost me when I was ready to quit, to spur me on when I needed to move forward and to show me the "lioness" birthed within me by the Lord. I could not "roar" this message to grandparents without your passion igniting my spirit.

Finally, to Sherry Schumann, I dedicate this book. Frequently, you were willing to lend an ear and share an encouraging thought when I needed it most. You were my writing guru. How I thank the Lord for your shining example of writing for Him.

"To our God and Father be glory for ever and ever. Amen."
PHILIPPIANS 4:23

CONTENTS

Introduction: An Urgent Message   *xiii*

Chapter One: The Calling   1

Chapter Two: The Dirt on You   15
    Key One: Surrender Your Heart to the Lord

Chapter Three: Be a Rudy   27
    Key Two: Read the Bible Daily

Chapter Four: Babushkas on Their Knees   41
    Key Three: Pray Fervently

Chapter Five: Running for Life   61
    Key Four: Pursue Healthy Relationships

Chapter Six: Is There a Doctor in the House?   79
    Key Five: Heal Broken Relationships

Chapter Seven: Pencils, Notebooks, and Computers   99
    Key Six: Leave a Written Legacy of Love

Chapter Eight: Tell Your Stories   125
    Key Seven: Pass Your Faith

Chapter Nine: Make a Plan 143

Chapter Ten: Run, Grandparent, Run 155

Appendix A: SPACEPETS: An Acronym
　　for Personal Application of Biblical Truths 167

Appendix B: Conversation Starters for
　　Pursuing Healthy Relationships 171

Appendix C: Prayer for the Salvation of a
　　Grandchild 173

Appendix D: Blessings Recorded in Scripture 175

Appendix E: Tips for Sharing the Gospel
　　with Children 177

Endnotes *179*

INTRODUCTION

AN URGENT MESSAGE

Dear Grandparent,

Did you know that you could become a life changer for your grandchildren? In fact, that is God's vision for all grandparents. In Psalm 78:4, we are told to "tell the next generation the praiseworthy deeds of the Lord." In a world rampant with terrorist attacks and police shootings, such words are life-giving. Our grandchildren navigate a world that is caustic to God's ways. Sharing with them the Good News of Jesus Christ can change the trajectory of their lives not only eternally but also daily.

The purpose of this book is to examine seven key principles that will equip you to significantly impact your grandchildren. By leading your loved ones into a meaningful relationship with the Lord, you create a legacy more valuable than real estate or money. You pass on a legacy of faith. It is grandparenting that makes a difference.

We Baby Boomers have reached our fifth, sixth, or seventh decade of life. Even though we may have been passionate about serving the Lord in the 1960s, many of us have cooled down. We have become complacent. We have retired from our jobs, and, unfortunately, too many of us have retired from our spiritual calling.

But that is not the heart of God. His plan, as stated in 2 Timothy 4:7, is that we fight "the good fight," finish "the race," and keep "the faith" until He takes us home to heaven. There is no retirement in God's kingdom.

Over eighty million grandparents live in the United States. We have the potential to change the direction of not only our families but also our country. If one million grandparents took a stand by fighting "the good fight," we could make a powerful impact. Revival could come.

Like many Baby Boomers, I struggled to be the godly grandmother God purposed for me. As I sought His wisdom, He revealed seven keys that encouraged, informed, and equipped me to share God's love with my family. The first three keys focused on equipping my heart to reach my grandchildren's hearts. The remaining four keys concentrated on specific tools that enabled me to fulfill this God-given opportunity to change the lives of my loved ones.

In our spiritually corrosive culture, God is calling all grandparents to be life changers. He yearns for us to make a difference in these treacherous times by passing a legacy of faith in Jesus Christ to our grandchildren. Never has there been a more important job to do. Never has the need been more urgent.

For eternity together,
Catherine H. Jacobs
passthelegacy.com

"Tell it to your children, and let your children tell it to their children, and their children to the next generation."

JOEL 1:3

CHAPTER ONE

THE CALLING

My Story

What began as a typical summer morning quickly turned memorable. With an extensive list of errands stuffed into my purse, I jumped into my car and started the engine. As I exited the driveway, the distinctive jingle of my cell phone broke the silence in the car. I answered it in time to hear the familiar voice of Nate, my son-in-law. "Nina, are you ready to become a grandma today?"

Excited, I turned the car around and returned home. Once inside my house, I grabbed a prepared tote bag. Back in my car, I sped to the hospital. I barged into the maternity ward out of breath. I arrived in time … to wait.

My watch seemed to tick slowly as I spent the day in the waiting room. In the wee hours of the next morning, Nathaniel Dustin Davis was born. Cradling him for the first time, I understood he was special, but I did not know him yet. I wondered,

Who are you, Nathaniel? Will you be tall like your dad or artistic like your mom? Will you love to throw a football, or will you prefer computers? Then another question arose: *Who are you, Cathy, now that you are a grandmother?*

That morning I realized I was unprepared to be a grandmother.

When I was a child, only my maternal grandfather was living. He died when I was six years old. Therefore, I do not have many fond memories of spending time with my grandparents. I had no role model for this senior role of grandparenting.

After Nathaniel was born, I tried to be the best grandma I could be. I cooked dinners, babysat, and bought diapers when they were on sale. Within a few months, though, I felt drained. Could there be more to the grandparent role than I thought?

Perplexed, I sought guidance from the Lord. I aspired to be a good grandparent, but soon I learned that God desires more than goodness. He wants godliness. His plan, as shown in Psalm 145:4, is for grandparents to tell the next generation about His mighty acts.

God's Calling

In many ways, our Western culture promotes the idea that when people reach the age of fifty-five or sixty, they are past their prime. It is time for them to step aside.

But moving aside is not God's plan.

Before the first flower bloomed on the face of this earth, the Creator of the heavens and earth fashioned all people. Carefully knitting together each one, He had a unique purpose in mind for each person, which aligned with His overarching mission: to raise a people for Him to love, who would return that love to Him.

God's destiny for His people has always been for us to be actively engaged in life. In Hebrews 12:1, we are told to "run with perseverance the race marked out for us." We are to run this race of life until we take our final breath.

Retirement does not exist in God's kingdom.

You may have many grandchildren. Maybe these children live down the street, or maybe they live across the country. You may be a grandparent-in-waiting, that is, waiting for your grown children to get married and have children. Or you may be a special, nonbiological grandparent who has a caring relationship with a particular child in your neighborhood or church.

Regardless of which category fits you, God has called you for "such a time as this" (Esther 4:14). You were not called to grandparent a hundred years ago during the dark days of World War I. Nor are you expected to grandparent a hundred years into the future. You have been called to grandparent in the early decades of the twenty-first century.

God's Destiny for You

The specifics of God's destiny for you are between the Lord and you. But certainly God has placed at the top of each grandparent's list the assignment of passing a legacy of faith in His Son, Jesus Christ, to his or her grandchildren. If you are a person of faith, you hold within your heart the treasure of the Good News of Jesus Christ. This news impacts life today and for eternity. By sharing Jesus Christ with your loved ones, you are equipping them to live life at its best.

God intentionally placed each child or grandchild in your life, whether they are biological or nonbiological. Having these

3

special people in your life is an honor. In fact, impacting the next generation for the sake of Jesus Christ is a sacred trust the almighty God has given to us. He planned for you to pour your heart into your loved ones as you share the wisdom you have gained from your experiences. Often, these truths cannot be learned from a book, a peer, or a parent.

The Lord planned for you to share these truths so you can help to guide the hearts of these loved ones. They live in a challenging world. Each child needs to hear that God created him, loves him, and has an amazing plan for his life. What better person to pass these truths to that child than the grandparent who loves him or her? As designed by God, biblical discipleship means we are called to disciple the next generation to become lifelong followers of Jesus Christ. The goal is for all of us to arrive home in heaven for eternity.

The Problem We Face

However, some of us have encountered a formidable problem. Our grown children and grandchildren have left the church—the church family that helped to raise them. Leaving the church building is not the root problem, though. The tragedy is that our loved ones have walked away from their faith in Christ. They have severed their relationship with their heavenly Father, and they are walking through life alone.

Grandparents struggle with this issue because, in many cases, we did all we knew to do to raise our children in the faith. We followed the model given to us. At some point, we embraced the faith, but our children have not. We feel sad, guilty, confused.

Influential, Unbiblical Worldviews

Our children and grandchildren do not embrace faith in Christ as we did for several reasons. Most of these reasons are connected to the powerful impact our troubled culture has on them. It encourages future generations of our families to have worldviews contrary to the Bible. In fact, three major worldviews drive a wedge between our children and the Lord.

The first is relativism. This philosophy says truth is relative; therefore there is no absolute truth. In the past, we as a nation embraced certain truths whether or not we called ourselves Christians. As a culture, we all believed that murder, theft, and premarital sex (to name a few) were wrong. But today, our culture views these previously absolute truths as relative. Instead, the view is that each person is the designer of truth as he or she sees it. What I think to be true is true for me. What you think to be true is true for you. This relativism heavily influences our children's faith in God. Rather than easily following our example of being followers of Jesus Christ, our loved ones hesitate, question, and seek other gods to follow.

A second worldview caustic to faith in Jesus Christ is pluralism. This philosophy promotes the idea that there are many ways to the truth—whatever the truth might be for you. No one way is superior to another. Each individual must determine which way is authentic for him. Faith in Christ may be true for us. However, many of our loved ones do not believe such faith is a valid belief for them.

This is not a new way of thinking. In fact, Jesus encountered it in His time on earth. That is why He said, "I am the way, and the truth, and the life. No man comes to the Father [that is God] except through me" (John 14:6). He was declaring that there are not many ways to truth. There is only one way—through Him.

Extreme tolerance is a third worldview contradictory to biblical thinking. Today people are expected to accept whatever views or lifestyles their families, neighbors, and society maintain. Each person's worldview is considered equally reasonable. We are to be the authors of our own views. Even if someone else's values conflict with ours, we are expected to be open-minded, allowing each person to live as he or she sees fit. Our loved ones may ask themselves why parents or grandparents should tell their children or grandchildren how to live.

The result of these pervasive modern worldviews is that many of our youths have walked away from the Lord. Barna Group, a private, nonpartisan, for-profit organization under the Issachar Companies, states "that nearly six in ten (59%) young people who grow up in Christian churches end up walking away."[1] Statistically speaking, this means six out of ten high school seniors who were involved with the church in high school will abandon their relationship with the Lord. The Nehemiah Institute puts the percentage higher: They say, "Upwards of 70% of youth from Christian homes attending public schools cease attending church after high school."[2]

Is There Hope?

Many grandparents have heavy hearts when they read such statistics. We are troubled and broken as we watch our loved ones walk away from the Lord.

Is there hope?

Is there anything we can do to point the hearts of our children and grandchildren toward the Lord?

Yes. There is tremendous hope for our families—that is, if you and I become proactive to pass faith in Jesus Christ to the next generation. God has given grandparents a power of influence over the hearts and minds of our grandchildren that is second only to their parents.

Think about this: God designed you for this job of reaching future generations for Him. You have a God-designed, God-given power of influence over your loved ones that is unparalleled. In no way does this diminish the importance of pastors, Sunday school teachers, or youth leaders. But our influence to connect the hearts of our children and grandchildren with the Lord's heart is primary.

God's plan has always been for parents and grandparents to encourage godly faith in their children and grandchildren, regardless of their age. Even when our children and grandchildren are grown, we continue to be their parents or grandparents. As time passes, we go through seasons of life. We do not parent or grandparent a fifteen-year-old the way we did when he was five years old. Similarly, we relate differently to a thirty-five-year-old son than to a twenty-year-old son. But we have a godly influence over their hearts until we leave this earthly life.

The Call to Fight the Good Fight

We accept the job God has given us: to reach the hearts and minds of our loved ones in the generation that follows ours. Then we can link arms with this next generation to raise the youngest generation to know, love, and serve the Lord Jesus Christ.

But how do we reach our families for the Lord?

Most Christian Baby Boomers long to connect the hearts of their loved ones with the Lord. But many grandparents are floundering. We feel unprepared for such a task. We simply do not know how to encourage faith in our children and grandchildren.

Grandparents, please understand that you do not stand alone in this task. When God calls someone, He promises to be there every step of the way. Isaiah 41 says that God called us from the "farthest corners" of the earth and He will "strengthen" us: He will uphold us with His "righteous right hand" (vv. 9–10).

Also, when Jesus delivered the Great Commission in Matthew 28:18–20, He told His disciples that "all authority in heaven and on earth has been given to me." Then He commissioned them to "go and make disciples of all nations." This calling to make disciples of all nations starts at home. As grandparents, our children and grandchildren are our first mission field. Jesus' final words were that He would be with the disciples "always, to the very end of the age."

No, grandparents are never alone in the task of impacting the hearts and lives of their families.

Spiritual Attack

The spiritual attack on the hearts and minds of our loved ones is far worse than any attack by ISIS, Russia, or Afghanistan. We have an Enemy who does not fight fairly. Ephesians 6:12 states, "Our struggle is not against flesh and blood, but against the rulers, against the authorities, against the powers of this dark world and against the spiritual forces of evil in the heavenly realms." These spiritual forces of evil are mighty. They are beyond our human ability to overcome. But God assures us in 1 John 4:4 that "the one who is in you is greater than the one who is in the world." We have available to us the most formidable power of all to combat the worldly influences impacting the faith and lives of our loved ones.

So much is at stake. We need every grandfather and grandmother to stand up and join the army of grandparents passing a legacy of faith in Jesus Christ to their loved ones. Truly, this is "the good fight" Paul referred to in 2 Timothy 4:7. We fight by keeping our personal faith strong as we run the race of life God has placed before us. We are to run diligently in the power of His grace until we take our final breath.

An Earthly Memory of a Heavenly Truth

I remember running across my uncle's farmyard one day when I was five years old. Minutes earlier my family had arrived at his house. The sun was bright. It was probably hot, too, there in the heart of South Carolina. I do not remember the heat, though. I only recall the bright sunshine of the day. The crops stood on both sides of the beaten-down dirt path that ran from my uncle's house to my granddaddy's house. The crops were probably cotton, but I paid no attention to them. I was focused on the "big house" ahead—and on my granddaddy. He lived in that wood-framed house. Eagerly, I raced up the steps and onto the wraparound porch. Huge pecan trees offered their shade on the far side of this veranda. He sat in the shadows of the pecan grove. Watching, waiting, he was longing for me to come to him. As he pulled me onto his lap, I smelled the sweetness of peppermint. He always had peppermint sticks in his pocket. He wrapped his long arms around me and shared his sweet treats with me. We sat there, rocking together.

That memory depicts a snapshot of life—that is, an earthly picture of a heavenly truth. Just as my granddaddy watched, waited, and longed for me to come to him, so, too, does the grandest daddy of all watch, wait, and long for us to come to Him. On life's journey, we are all running to our Daddy in His heavenly home. We have the open invitation to develop an intimate relationship with Him in order to do life with Him—both for today and forever.

That is why you and I, as grandparents, have been called by our heavenly Father to point the hearts of our children and grandchildren toward the heart of their heavenly Father. We have been asked by God to tell these precious people about their wonderful Daddy in heaven (see Psalm 145:4). This amazing Father chose them, loves them, and has an incredible plan for their lives.

Leaving a Legacy

Each of us will leave a legacy. The question is, what kind of legacy will we leave our children, grandchildren, and great-grandchildren? Certainly, God intends for it to be more than real estate or money. If we are not intentional, prayerful, and careful, we will leave a diminished, compromised legacy. Therefore, we must rise to the calling God has placed on our lives and pass a God-centered legacy.

Is there breath in you? Then know that God has a plan for you.

With great joy, in the following chapters I share with you The Seven Keys the Lord revealed to me. May they empower each of you to step out boldly in faith and counter the anti-biblical worldviews that have a powerful, ungodly impact on the lives of your loved ones. With these keys, you may touch the hearts of your family members and become a life changer for them. Prepare to run an astonishing race with the Lord by your side. Pursue His calling to you as you pass a legacy of faith in Jesus Christ to your loved ones.

Yes, we can be grandparents who make a difference. There is no higher calling. There is no greater legacy.

Study Questions

Chapter One: The Calling

Pounding It Out

1. What does being a good grandparent mean to you? Is this the same as being a godly grandparent? If not, what is the difference?

2. Read Hebrews 12:1–2. What does Paul say about "running the race"? In your opinion, what is retirement? Did people "retire" a hundred years ago? Why or why not? Do you think retirement is a biblical or a cultural concept?

3. Write what you think is God's purpose for the season in life that our culture calls retirement.

4. What are three worldviews that are contrary to biblical thinking? [Relativism, pluralism, tolerance] Do you see how these secular worldviews impact your children? Grandchildren? Give a few examples.

5. What is a legacy? What kind of legacy are you leaving your loved ones? Are you leaving a spiritual heritage?

6. God in His wisdom created parents and grandparents to have a God-designed power of influence over their children and grandchildren. How does this agree or disagree with the beliefs and practices of our culture?

Driving It Home

1. Do you think God intended for your godly influence over your children and grandchildren to end once they become adults? Does it change? How? When?
2. What kind of amazing purpose do you think God called you to be as a godly grandparent? Write down this purpose and post on your bathroom mirror so you can contemplate it frequently.

THE DIRT ON YOU

Key One: Surrender Your Heart to the Lord

When we agonize over our loved ones, often it is the Holy Spirit tugging at our hearts. Along with their parents, we are the ones God designed to point the hearts of our grandchildren toward Him. As an omniscient God, He knows everything. He sees the end from the beginning. He stirs within us awareness that all is not well, but we must allow the Lord to guide us in our efforts to reach the hearts of our grandchildren. We do not want to be meddling grandparents. Instead, we want to be led by the Holy Spirit.

The first step to grandparents making a difference is to examine our heart connection with the Lord. Is it strong? Is it healthy? Is it intimate? Before we speak a word to our grandson or granddaughter, we should speak first to the Lord. All too often, the ways of the world creep into our lives and challenge our relationship with the Lord. For the sake of our grandchildren, we need to surrender our hearts to Christ.

The Call to Surrender

Surrender is a challenging word. We bristle at the thought of humbling ourselves before anyone, especially before an invisible god. Yet surrender is an important step if we desire to become close to the Lord. Once I heard a young pastor define surrender in a way that made the concept easier for me to embrace. He said, "Surrendering to God is allowing Him to come into your life and mess with it."[3] To surrender is to give the Lord permission to make changes in our lives. We acquiesce so Jesus can guide us with His wisdom for His purposes. We let go of the way the world encourages us to live, and we choose to live according to God's plans. We lay aside our agendas, release our independence, and take up God's purposes by relying on Him.

Deuteronomy 6:5 tells us to "love the Lord your God with all your heart, and with all your soul and with all your strength." Moses spoke those words to the people of Israel as part of his final instructions before they entered the land promised to their forefathers.

Jesus used similar wording when a religious leader asked Him what was the "great commandment in the Law" (Matthew 22:36). Jesus replied with the mighty words of Moses: "Love the Lord your God with all your heart and with all your soul and with all your mind" (v. 37).

We cannot love God with our own strength. Instead, we need God to help us get to Him. When we earnestly seek Him, God will open the way for us to intimately love Him. Jeremiah 29:13 says, "You will seek me and find me when you seek me with *all* your heart" (emphasis added). The next verse says, "'I will be found by you,' declares the Lord." Hebrews 11:6 reminds us that God "rewards those who earnestly seek him."

Before we can extricate our grandchildren from the clutches of this world, we must first run to the Lord, earnestly seeking Him with all our heart. For some, this may mean praying for the first time and inviting the Lord Jesus to come into your life.

Perhaps you have attended church all of your life. But if you have never surrendered your heart to God, then speak to the Lord today, confessing your sins and offering Him your life. This prayer is critical. It is important not only for your own heart but also for the hearts of your family members. When you ask Jesus to come into your life, He transforms you into a godly vessel that He can use. (See Prayer of Commitment in the study questions at the end of this chapter.)

On the other hand, you may have invited Jesus into your life years ago. If so, then you should be pursuing spiritual growth—the journey of becoming more like Jesus. Ask Him to purify your life by drawing you close to Him. Seek to lean on Him in every aspect of your life—especially for leading your grandchildren to Him. (See Prayer of Recommitment in the study questions at the end of this chapter.)

Three Categories of People

The Old Testament tells the story of God's chosen people, the Israelites, leaving Egypt, a land where they had been slaves for many generations. They headed toward Canaan, the land promised to their ancestors. As they marched toward this glorious land that is rich in resources, they failed to follow the ways of God. Instead, they focused on their self-centered desires. The result is that they wandered in the desert for forty years, often going in circles—literally. They finally reached Canaan where they lived according to the promises of God.

Spiritually speaking, we are like the Israelites. Even though they lived hundreds of years ago, we can use their seasons of life to identify three categories of people. Some people live in a spiritual Egypt, where they are enslaved or attached to the ways of the world. Some people wander in the desert, walking in circles as they attempt to follow God but often resort to relying on their own wisdom. Others live in the Promised Land. They daily seek to follow the ways of God.

Throughout my childhood and early teens, I spiritually lived in Egypt. In college, I began to ask questions about the meaning of life. During my senior year, a close friend asked me, "If you died tonight, do you know for certain that you would go to heaven?"

I could not answer yes.

Shortly after that conversation, I started to attend various Bible studies. Through many late-night conversations with Christian friends, I learned firsthand about a personal relationship with the Lord. For a few months, similar to the Israelites, I wandered in circles.

One Sunday I went to my home church and knelt on a prayer pillow. I prayed silently and asked the Lord to come into my life. There were no flashing lights or ringing bells. But weeks later, I realized my life had changed. My relationship with God was different. He had truly become my Lord and savior.

Decades have passed since that morning. How thankful I am for the Lord's residence in my heart so that, by His grace, I may abide in the Promised Land of continual fellowship with Him. I cherish His presence in my life. As I purpose to point the hearts of my loved ones toward the Lord, I know it is His resounding truth that shines through my surrendered heart. Repeatedly, I lay down my life for Him to use. I cannot lead my children and grandchildren through my own abilities. I can only guide these precious people toward the Lord as I am empowered by Him.

Which group describes your life? Are you in Egypt being pulled and swayed by the ways of our culture? Are you in the desert, wandering in circles, conflicted about following God? Perhaps you are in the Promised Land, relying on the promises of God, living in continual fellowship with Him. Honestly evaluate your life. If you are not living in the Promised Land, ask the Lord to bring you into it. As you draw near to God, you will be empowered by the Holy Spirit to pour truth into your grandchildren's lives.

The Need for Forgiveness

In Chapter One, you read about my granddaddy. He watched, waited, and longed for his granddaughter to visit him. As he sat on his front porch, he scrutinized every car that passed. Can you imagine the joy in his heart when the right car finally passed his house? Soon he saw me running down the path. His heart pounded faster as little Cathy climbed the porch steps and jumped onto his lap. Why did he sit on the edge of his chair waiting for me to come? He loved me. He craved to spend time with me.

Our heavenly Father also waits and longs for us to come to Him. He loves us. Zephaniah 3:17 says that He delights in us. Imagine the God of the Universe receiving joy from being with you and with me. We mean the world to Him.

When you think about this loving Father, does your heart swell? Do you aspire to step closer to Him? Who in your life has been special to you? Maybe you desire to share a cup of coffee with your daughter. Or is it that dear grandchild who makes your heart burst with joy? Keep these images in your heart. Use them as motivation to draw near each day to the One who rejoices "over you with singing" (Zephaniah 3:17).

A significant part of surrendering our lives to Christ is seeking His forgiveness for anything we may have done to separate us from God. We live in a broken and sinful world. Each one of us falls short of God's best for us (Romans 3:23). Each of us gives in to sin.

Do not let the word *sin* offend you. It is a word we may hear often but do not understand fully. Sin is anything we say, do, or think that separates us from God. God is holy. He is perfect in every way. He cannot associate with anything that is not perfect. If He did, He would be contaminated with unholiness and therefore would no longer be perfect. As the Holy God, He must draw the line and separate Himself.

To impact the hearts of our grandchildren spiritually, we must be purified of our sinfulness—our unholiness. We cannot remove this spiritual dirt by ourselves. When we ask God to forgive us, He is faithful to wash us clean (1 John 1:9). We can then become a powerful voice for Him. The Holy Spirit flows into our hearts and enables us to be grandparents who make a difference in the lives of our grandchildren.

The Need for Cleansing

When I was a little girl, my family moved to a new neighborhood. Across the street lived a boy named Johnny. We played together often. Our moms both instructed us that one of them had to accompany us if we wanted to cross the street. One day Johnny and I wanted to play, but our moms were busy. We bantered back and forth as to which mom we should bother. Johnny, disgusted, started walking toward his house. I yelled for him to stop, but he ignored me. I yelled again. He continued to walk. I studied the street. Then I did the forbidden thing: I ran across the street to play with him.

Johnny, feeling a bit smug, started walking down the sidewalk. A second strict mom-rule was that we had to stay in our yards. Johnny passed the boundary of his yard. Not to be left behind, I ran after him, trying to bring him back to our mom-approved playground. Johnny kept walking. Finally, he stopped near a construction site, where a house was being built.

Earlier in the week, crews had prepped this property for the foundation, but several days of rain had interrupted the work. Deep holes had been dug in the North Carolina red mud. After a brief pause, Johnny walked down the muddy embankment and stood at the edge of the freshly dug cavern. I followed him. We stood there for a few minutes, gazing into the muddy pit.

What happened next might be a point of controversy. But I will stand by my side of the story. Johnny pushed me into that muddy, red clay. He then ran off, leaving me in my shame and horror. I pulled myself out of the mud. I was a mess. Covered from head to toe with deep-red clay, I started home, crying the entire way.

As I walked up our driveway, I looked toward the house and saw the curtains of the front room flutter. But I ignored it. As I rounded the rear corner of our house, the back door opened. There appeared my mother, standing tall and serene. Firmly, she inquired, "Where have you been?"

Sobbing at this point, I could barely speak. Somehow I managed to tell her the horrible story. As I finished, I moved toward the house. Mother swiftly stepped in between the doorway and me. "You cannot go inside the house," she said. "You are dirty. My house is clean." She paused for a moment, then continued, "But you wait here."

She went inside the house. A few minutes later, she reappeared with some towels. My mom knelt beside me. Calmly, but grimly, she stripped me of my outer clothes, hair bow, socks, and shoes. She took me by the hand and led me to the backyard faucet. She turned the knob on the spigot, and picking up the hose, she slowly rinsed the mud off me. Some of the red clay resisted the water spray. But my mother persevered. Eventually, I was clean. My mom gently wrapped a fuzzy towel around me. Cradling me in her arms, she whispered into my ear, "Now you can come into my house."

Because I disobeyed my mother, I became physically covered with dirt. Similarly, because we have disobeyed God, our hearts are covered with sin. The dirt in my story was mud, the kind that clings tightly. Sin is like that. It sticks like glue to your heart. Some sins are more easily removed than others. To enter God's kingdom—His heavenly home that is perfect in every way—we must be thoroughly cleansed. As my mother took me by the hand to be washed, the Holy Spirit can lead us to a place of cleansing. After my mother washed me, she wrapped her loving arms around me and carried me into her home. So, too, Jesus can wrap His loving arms around us to carry us into His Kingdom. As my mother watched for me to come home, Jesus stands waiting for us to come to Him.

Do you long for your grandchildren to know, love, and serve the Lord? You have the God-given power to be a life changer for them, to be a grandparent who makes a difference. Run to Him. Surrender to Him. Ask Him to cleanse you of all the dirtiness in your life. It is the first key in passing a legacy of faith to future generations.

Key One: Surrender Your Heart to the Lord

"If we confess our sins, he is faithful and just and will forgive us our sins and purify us from all unrighteousness."

1 JOHN 1:9

"If you declare with your mouth, 'Jesus is Lord,' and believe in your heart that God raised him from the dead, you will be saved."

ROMANS 10:9

Study Questions

Chapter Two: The Dirt on You

Pounding It Out

1. Did you raise your children in the church? How many of these "churched" youth walk with the Lord today?
2. If you have an angst within your spirit concerning your grown children or grandchildren, what is the first step you should take to deal with this concern? [Surrender your heart to Christ]
3. Catherine defined surrender as "letting go of the way the world encourages us to live by making the choice to live according to God's plans." What do you think of this definition?

    a. Write your own definition of *surrender*.
    b. According to your definition, have you surrendered your heart to Christ? If not, would you like to do so today? (See Prayer of Commitment and Prayer of Recommitment at the end of this chapter).

4. What three types of people are presented in this chapter? [Those living in Egypt, those wandering in the desert, and those abiding in the Promised Land]. Which type are you? What can you do to become a person who abides in the Promised Land?
5. What is sin? [Sin is anything we say, do, or think that separates us from God] What does Romans 3:23 say about sin? In her story, Catherine says sin sticks to a

person like mud. Can we cleanse ourselves from this dirt? [No] How do you get clean before God? [Repent by acknowledging your sin, then ask God to cleanse you].

6. Are you willing to do whatever it takes to fight for the hearts and minds of your loved ones? If you are not willing, then who do you think will accept that responsibility?

Driving It Home

1. Picture Catherine's granddaddy waiting and watching for her. Can you picture your heavenly "daddy" waiting and watching for you? Do you think He is waiting for your grown kids? Your grandkids? What can you do to point their hearts toward their heavenly daddy?
2. Just as Catherine's mother stood waiting for her to come home, Jesus now waits for us to come to Him, talk to Him, be cleansed by Him, and seek His heart. Use one of the following prayers to surrender your heart to Christ. This is the first step in connecting your loved ones with the Lord.

Prayer of Commitment

Dear Lord Jesus, I ask that You come into my heart to live forever. I invite You into my life as my Lord and Savior. You died for me, and now I want to live for You. Please help me to never allow the things of this world to draw me away from You. Please forgive me of my sins and help me to follow You all the days of my life. In Jesus' name, amen.

Prayer of Recommitment

My Father God, the day salvation was offered to me was the day my life truly began. I recommit my life to you now as Your child, claiming You again as my Lord and Savior. Please forgive me of any sin or darkness that may be lurking in my heart. Fill me now so I may be full of Your Holy Spirit and live an empowered life for You. In the name of Jesus I pray, amen.

A Prayer for Your Family

Dear Jesus, may my every word and deed reflect that I am a new creation based only on the redemption I have received from You. Help me, Father, to be a living example of You. Let me not ever be tempted to turn away from You or take my eyes off You, the Savior who died for me. I ask for Your help, both for my loved ones and for me, that our lives may reflect You. Hold us, dear Father, in the palms of Your hands, where nothing can upset or distract us from Your plan. Guide us by Your Holy Spirit through this life. In Your name we pray, amen.

CHAPTER THREE

BE A RUDY

Key Two: Read the Bible Daily

Recently, I experienced the pleasure of FaceTime with all my grown children. Since we are scattered across the East Coast, being together is a rarity. My sons arranged a FaceTime family gathering on a Sunday evening. Meanwhile, I texted all my kids and told them to mark their calendars as the Jacobs were meeting face-to-face. At 8:00 p.m., I hit the link my son Chris sent me. Voilà! I saw his face. Over the next few minutes, the others joined. Soon my entire family was online together.

I started the conversation by asking one son a couple of questions. A few minutes later, I asked another one some questions. Quickly, the dialogue between my family members sprang forward. At that point, I reclined in my chair, listening to these siblings and their spouses chat, laugh, and poke fun at each other. With their faces scattered across my computer screen, I was thrilled to watch my loved ones interact with each other. For over an hour, I basked in the joy of their company.

The next morning, I thanked the Lord for the opportunity to visit with my children. What a treasured evening it had been. Then I remembered a Bible verse I often use as I begin my time with the Lord. I turned my Bible to Zephaniah 3:17: "The Lord your God is with you, he is mighty to save. He will take *great delight* in you, he will quiet you with his love, he will rejoice over you with singing" (NIV 1984 edition, emphasis added).

In the past, I had struggled with the thought that the Lord delighted in me. I questioned if He actually enjoyed my presence. But that morning, for the first time, I understood His joy. Just as I delighted in spending time with my children, my heavenly Father delights in spending time with me. Imagine that! The Lord of the universe loves my company, and I love to read His Word because it fills His heart with joy.

Living in the twenty-first century, many of us lead hectic lives. Often we are overcommitted and exhausted. Wisely, God tells us, "Be *still* and *know* that I am God" (Psalm 46:10, emphasis added). One way to apply this verse is to read the Bible daily so God can strengthen our spirits and equip us to navigate this frenetic world.

A Lesson from Rudy

When my daughter, Carrie, married years ago, we spent much time together planning her wedding and reception. It was mother-daughter time I will always treasure. As her special day grew closer, Carrie worried that I would be lonely and sad after the wedding. Because she is an attentive daughter, she decided to remedy the situation by giving me a Yorkshire puppy. How surprised I was on Christmas morning when Rudy leapt out of her arms and into my heart. Life has not been the same.

A few years later, I was in the midst of a difficult divorce. Broken to the core, I felt depressed and hopeless. One Saturday morning, I gathered my Bible and journal to go before the Lord and seek His help. As usual, Rudy followed me into the study. I settled quickly. But Rudy did not. Bored with my stillness, he ran to get his ball. Playfully, he dropped the toy at my feet. He barked, wagged his tail, and waited eagerly for me to join the game. He barked again when I ignored him. I told him sharply, "Be quiet." When he continued begging for my participation, I put the little gray doggie outside. Finally, the room was quiet.

One hour slipped by. Then two hours passed. I neared the end of this time with the Lord. Feeling guilty about Rudy, I let him inside, then returned to the chair to conclude my quiet time.

Rudy was ecstatic. He ran around the room. This time, intrigued, I watched this bundle of boundless energy. After circumnavigating the room, he jumped several times before landing in the chair next to me. Pausing for a few seconds, he got up and plopped on top of my feet. Turning his head slowly, he studied me with his dark eyes. With concentrated intention, the fluffy puppy leapt onto my lap, which was filled with books, journals, and pencils. How he found a free space to land, I do not know. But he did. With a quiet sigh, my little Rudy settled down, content to be close to me.

During the next few moments, I asked the Lord, "What can I do to follow You? I'm devastated. How can I find the strength and courage to take the next step?" Life loomed large and my circumstances seemed scary. Tearfully, I lowered my head in helplessness.

In the depth of my sorrow and brokenness, the Lord spoke gently to me, "Cathy, be a Rudy."

I looked at the furry ball curled up in a tiny space among the books on my lap.

"What, Lord?"

"Be a Rudy!"

"How, Lord? What do I do?"

"When life is tough, run toward me. Come near. If you continue to struggle, move closer. Sit at my feet. If that is not enough, my dearest, jump onto my lap. There is always room for you, my precious daughter."

An Invitation from the Lord

Many years have passed since that memorable Saturday. Numerous times I have heard the Lord's words in my heart: "Be a Rudy!" Each time I realize the Lord is wooing me—inviting me to come near—to sit at His feet or jump onto His lap.

In our fast-paced world, many voices call to us. We are often lured into multiple commitments and activities. Our culture shouts at us to "do." We are misled into thinking that our importance is defined by what we accomplish. This cultural mind-set of "doing" is the antithesis of God's desire for us to "be." We must stand against these lies and run daily to be a Rudy.

Being a Rudy means to draw near to the Lord. As grandparents, this Rudy principle is an important step toward passing a legacy of faith in Jesus Christ to the next generation. If we desire to impact the hearts and lives of our children and grandchildren for the Lord, we need to pursue with intentionality our intimate relationship with Him. The first key for Godly grandparenting is to surrender your "all" to Him. The second key is to read your Bible daily. People often refer to this daily reading of the Bible as a quiet time.

Countless books, studies, and videos are available to encourage us in our relationship with the Lord. Many are excellent resources. But it is vital for us to go first to the Bible, God's Word. In his gospel, the apostle John tells us about the "Word" becoming flesh. We learn that Jesus is the "living Word." The Bible is the written record of God sending His only son, Jesus, to us so we may live intimately with Him.

The Bible is unchanging and infallible. This book, composed of sixty-six smaller books, is different from every other book. Other manuscripts contain the ideas of people. Even though God used different authors to write His book, the words are not their own. The words are the thoughts of God. It is His message to us. Nothing in the Bible was created by man. God's Holy Spirit guided each person in all that he wrote. God explains in 2 Timothy 3:16-17 that "All Scripture is God-breathed and is useful for teaching, rebuking, correcting, and training in righteousness, so that the servant of God may be thoroughly equipped for every good work." These are God's words to us, His children. From Genesis to Revelation, it is one story written by one divine author.

Our heavenly Father loves for us to be with Him. His relationship with us is precious to Him. When we are still before Him in a quiet time, we choose to put the world behind us.

During this daily pause, God is able to speak to us through the Bible. At this point, two things happen. First, we get to know Him. We learn His personality, His desires, His ways. Second, He equips us to live the life He designed for us. Consequently, we become a role model to our loved ones as God envisioned.

Reading the Bible every day is crucial. Just as resting nightly strengthens our physical bodies, resting daily in God's Word strengthens our inner spirit. If we miss an hour or two of sleep, we become tired, maybe even exhausted, the next day. It is hard to do life. Also, by missing sleep, we compromise our health and make ourselves vulnerable to sickness. Similarly, if we miss a day or two of reading the Bible, we become tired spiritually. The ways of this world become attractive, even enticing. Our spiritual health also suffers, and we become easy targets for the Enemy. Reading the Bible daily is one of the best ways to arm ourselves against the Enemy and to protect us from the lures of the world. The Bible is our sword (Ephesians 6:17), our lamp (Psalm 119:105), and our light (Psalm 119:105).

As you hide His Word in your heart daily, you experience the intimate relationship with the Lord needed to point the hearts of your loved ones toward their heavenly Father. You are positioning yourself to pass a legacy of faith in Christ to your family.

The Power of the Word of God

A few days ago, I woke up early in the morning. Fear overwhelmed me. My mind raced with the many obligations facing me. I had writing deadlines to honor, a presentation to prepare, business details for my ministry to consider, and finances to juggle. I tossed and turned in bed. Finally, the sun peeped through my window. I got out of bed wondering how I would manage.

After walking Rudy, I plopped into my chair. I knew I should read my Bible, but I wondered if I had time since I had so much work to do. Hesitantly, I reached for my Bible. I turned to the designated daily reading. There on the page were the beautiful words from Proverbs 3:5-6: "Trust in the Lord with all your heart, and lean not on your own understanding; in all your ways submit to him, and he will make your paths straight." Oh, how I needed to read those words that morning. I did not know they would be the reading for the day. But the Lord did. He knew the words He needed to share with me before I got out of bed. The living Word of God was living in my life.

But the story gets better. That night I spent time with my grandchildren. As I tucked my oldest grandson into bed, I sat beside him for a few minutes. He was reading a book.

"Nathaniel," I said, "what book are you reading?"

"*Star Wars*."

"I bet that's a good book. But have you read from your Bible today?"

Slowly, he shook his head no.

"You know the Lord loves to speak to you each day. One of the best ways He talks to us is through His Word, the Bible. This morning I was feeling very frightened about some of the problems in my life. I felt like I didn't have time to read my Bible. But I did. Do you know what my reading was?"

Again, Nathaniel shook his head no.

"It was from Proverbs 3:5-6, which says, 'Trust in the Lord

with all your heart and lean not on your understanding; in all your ways submit to him and he will make your paths straight.' Wasn't that a wonderful word from God? He knew how concerned I was. He used His Word to comfort and encourage me."

Over the next few minutes, we talked about Proverbs. The conversation was not long. But the Lord gave me the opportunity to plant a legacy seed that night on the benefit of reading the Bible.

Establish a Daily Appointment with God

Many people want to spend time in God's Word. However, they struggle with the logistics. I find it helpful to follow four practical steps.

First, determine a reading schedule that is realistic for your current lifestyle. I start by asking the Lord to design my reading time. Then I pick a time and place where I put aside the distractions of this world so I may quietly abide in God's presence. I strive to meet the Lord in this place at the same time every day to firmly develop the habit of daily Bible reading. To me, it is an appointment with God. I even mark it on my calendar. My goal is to come into the presence of the Almighty God.

Think about that for a moment.

Due to the crucifixion and resurrection of Jesus Christ, you and I can come directly into the throne room of heaven. We may be sitting in our homes, but by intentionally turning our hearts and thoughts toward the Lord, we come into His presence. Like Rudy, we sit at the feet of our master. How amazing is that?

I suggest you have your quiet time in a place where you can sit in a chair. This is not the time to lounge on the sofa or recline in bed. If I am too comfortable, I get sleepy or distracted. I have an appointment with *God*! I want to give Him my full attention.

The second step is to use a Bible that is easy to read and understand. My favorite one is the New International Version (NIV). A number of excellent Bible translations are available with a variety of helpful tools. You may want to use a study Bible or a devotional Bible. To enhance your understanding of the text, a study Bible contains notes along the sides of each page in columns or at the bottom of the page. A devotional Bible includes inspirational readings by various authors and scholars. These devotions may be designed specifically for women or men, parents or couples, children or teens. One of my favorite devotional Bibles is *The Grandmother's Bible*, an excellent source of encouragement for grandmas. Your pastor, Sunday school teacher, or a sales person at a Christian bookstore may be able to recommend a Bible best suited for you.

The third Bible reading step is to bring a notebook and a pen to your quiet place. I find it helpful to jot down thoughts that come to me as I spend time with the Lord. I also record specific words or phrases that seem significant to me as I read the Scriptures.

The fourth step is to develop a reading plan. Often I use a devotional book or a study guide to structure my quiet time. Various reading plans are available online or at a Christian bookstore. Although some plans guide you through the whole Bible in one year, one of my favorite plans is to read one psalm, one proverb, and one chapter of a New Testament and/or Old Testament book each day. Following this method, I taste different parts of the Bible. The important point is to establish structure so I do not flounder when I start my quiet time. The structure keeps me on a timely tract.

When I was a new Christian, I enjoyed reading the gospels. The gospels are the first four books of the New Testament: Matthew, Mark, Luke, John. These books are eyewitness accounts of Jesus' life. Each one teaches who Jesus is and what He taught. Even though I had grown up in the church, I did not know many details of Jesus' life. In fact, some of my knowledge was faulty. My pastor suggested I begin with Mark because it is the shortest gospel. John is considered the most comprehensive. You might want to start with Mark, too, but whatever method you follow, make sure it suits your schedule. Forty years later, I continue to read at least one gospel each year.

When reading my Bible, I use a simple method I named "The Three R's"—Read, wRite, and Respond. Before I open my Bible, I bow my head to pray. As I complete The Three R's, I bow my head again, ending my time with the Lord in prayer. My quiet time usually flows this way:

Pray: I invite the Holy Spirit to come and speak to me as I read. I say, "Show me what You want me to learn."

Read: I read the Scripture passage two times. The first time, I read it to myself. The second time, I sometimes read it aloud.

wRite: I summarize the passage in my own words and make special note of any words, phrases, or thoughts that impress me.

Respond: At this point, I ask myself, "How does this Scripture apply to me?"

Based on the passage, I write down at least one action step for me to incorporate into my life to be obedient to the passage.

Pray:

1. I thank the Lord for His Word and this teaching.
2. I ask the Lord to give me His power and grace to receive and respond to this lesson appropriately.
3. I remain still for a few minutes to let the words of the day's passage settle within my spirit and to let the Lord speak further to me.

Probing the Bible

A few years ago, Pastor Rick Warren posted on his website a teaching on studying the Bible. In this post, he offers eight questions that will deepen your time in God's Word. He calls it the "probe-it" method of Bible study. Like a jackhammer, these questions hit the scriptural text and prompt us to think about the meaning and application we may not recognize otherwise. These thought-provoking questions can easily be incorporated into the "Respond" level of The Three R's. See Appendix A for the complete list of questions.

A Trend

Sometimes I notice a trend in my quiet time. Maybe the trend includes a topic for me to contemplate—for example, forgiveness. Or it may be a certain activity or response, such as calling a family member or friend who needs encouragement. These thoughts become invaluable to me because they make my quiet time in God's Word applicable to my life. I specifically ask myself how to use these words or thoughts. Often the Holy Spirit is teaching me a lesson. I end my quiet time pondering these lessons, as they are the gold nuggets of my time with the Lord.

An Amazing Book

Yes, the Bible is an amazing book provided for us by God. It tells the most compelling story of all time, the story of the true God who longs to be with His people forever. He gave us this heavenly treasure so we can know how to run our earthly race. One day we will see Him face-to-face. But until then, let us draw near to Him daily by reading and rereading His written Word. Remember, He delights in you. You bring joy to His heart and a smile to His face when you choose to spend time with Him.

Are your grown children heavy on your heart? Do you have concerns for your grandchildren growing up in a world moving fast and furiously? If so, grab the second key to becoming a life changer. Run to the Lord. Be a Rudy. Open your Bible daily and read His Word.

Key Two: Read the Bible Daily

"Be still, and know that I am God."

PSALM 46:10

"Be still before the Lord and wait patiently for him."

PSALM 37:7

"Wait for the Lord; be strong and take heart and wait for the Lord."

PSALM 27:14

"Whatever was written in earlier times was written for our instruction, so that through perseverance and the encouragement of the Scriptures we might have hope."

ROMANS 15:4

Study Questions

Chapter Three: Be a Rudy

Pounding It Out

1. What is the Bible? [The unchanging, infallible Word of God] Why is it important to read and study God's written Word? [To guide and guard our hearts so we may live according to His purpose for our lives] How does this book differ from all other books? [Written by God to reveal to us His purpose and plans for our lives]

2. How do you feel when you have not received adequate physical rest? Why is it important to "rest" spiritually in God's Word every day? [To position ourselves so we may seek the Lord for His revelation to us]

3. Has there been a time or situation when the Bible really spoke to you? Describe what happened.

4. What is your favorite verse/passage? Why?

5. What is a quiet time? [Time spent quietly before the Lord, focusing on Him and His Word] Describe how you would like to spend your quiet time with the Lord.

Driving It Home

1. "Being a Rudy" means to run to the Lord, sit still at His feet, and, when necessary, jump onto His lap. How can you be a Rudy this week?

2. This week spend time each day being a Rudy. Take a notebook with you into this quiet time with the Lord. Follow The Three R's presented in this chapter as you read your Bible. Share with your group or a friend one action step revealed to you from this Bible reading.

CHAPTER FOUR

BABUSHKAS ON THEIR KNEES

Key Three: Pray Fervently

A few years ago, Joni Eareckson Tada traveled to Russia. While visiting this country, she met an old woman who cleaned the hotel lobby floors. Through an interpreter, Joni became friends with the elderly lady by praising her excellent care of the floor. The lady was aged and wrinkled but had bright-red cheeks that were framed by her colorful headscarf. She wore layers of skirts and leggings with boots. She had bright-blue eyes and a shiny, gold-toothed smile. Standing in the hotel lobby with her broom in hand, she seemed out of place. Joni felt perhaps that was what attracted her to the woman.

While in Russia, Joni also met other Russian babushkas. People call these women "the praying grandmothers." They were the rock-solid saints Stalin aimed to eliminate. He realized if he could dispense with these old women, he had the opportunity to influence the Russian youth. Stalin knew once he controlled the youth, he could command the country.

Praise God, Stalin failed. Thank the Lord for these praying grandmothers. In her devotion, "Crowns of Splendor" in *The Grandmother's Bible*, Joni states that the babushka grandmothers connected a generation lost to atheism to a new generation who are asking questions about Jesus.[4]

I wonder what it was like for these women in the 1930s and 1940s? They witnessed Stalin's army march into their small villages. Soldiers entered their homes and dragged away their sons and grandsons. As the babushkas watched their men physically forced out of town, I imagine they wondered if they would see their loved ones alive again. What kind of prayers do you think these women uttered as they fell to their knees that day? Did they send up a quick, fleeting prayer? Or did they devote themselves to an intense, desperate time of crying out to the Lord?

Babushka-Strong Prayers

The third key for grandparents making a difference in the lives of their children and grandchildren is fervent prayer. Through their prayers, the Russian babushkas built a "cocoon," a spiritual wall of protection, around their families and their country. Both their physical enemy and their spiritual enemy were diminished due to the prayer barricade constructed by these praying grandmothers. By praying fervently, their prayers were like an incubator that helped to shape a protective environment, making it more challenging for the Enemy to penetrate their lives.

Twenty-first-century grandparents can do the same. Undoubtedly, the days of Stalin were terrible. But we also live in a time of turbulent spiritual battles. Our children and grand-children desperately need the strong prayer coverings of their babushkas as they maneuver through a world that is hostile to God's ways. It is God's vision that you and I as grandparents take up this role and fall to our knees daily, storming the gates of heaven on behalf of our loved ones. By being fervent in their prayers, the Russian babushkas made a tremendous difference in the lives of their families, thus impacting generations to come. So, too, we can make a difference in the lives of our children, grandchildren and future generations. We cannot afford to miss this opportunity God had given us to wrap our "cocoons of prayers" around the hearts of our loved ones thus "incubating" them from the world. Ruthanne Garlock and Quin Sherrer say, "The seeds of prayer that we plant today can yield a harvest of blessing for years to come."[5]

Our enemies may take the form of terrorists, extreme politi-cal groups, unemployment, or inflation. But, as we discussed in Chapter One, Ephesians 6:12 explains whom we are truly fight-ing: "For our struggle is not against flesh and blood, but against the rulers, against the authorities, against the powers of this dark world and against the spiritual forces of evil in the heavenly realms." These enemies are certainly powerful. Yet Scripture emphatically states that "the one who is in you is greater than the one who is in the world" (1 John 4:4). Due to Jesus' death and resurrection, the victory is ours. But we must fight for it. Lillian Penner says there is an urgency to "stand in the gap" for the hearts, minds, and souls of our loved ones so they do not become victims of our culture.[6] Just as Esther stood in the gap for her people, so, too, must we stand in the gap for our children and grandchildren.

Cavin Harper says, "We are in a spiritual battle requiring spiritual weapons."[7] Babushka-strong prayers are such weapons. II Corinthians 10:3-4 says, "For though we live in the world, we do not wage war as the world does. The weapons we fight with are not the weapons of the world. On the contrary, they have divine power."

Praying for our grandson to have a good day at school is an important prayer. Asking the Lord to be with our adult child in a job interview is significant. Both prayers have a valid place in our prayer times with the Lord. But babushka-strong prayers are prayers of a higher calling that require a deeper level of conversation with the Lord. Becoming such a strong prayer warrior is a challenge. It is not for the fainthearted. Harper says, "It is for passionate, intentional grandparents who are willing to get on their knees daily to intercede and plead for their grandchildren's life and salvation."[8]

As I seek to be a godly grandmother, I hear the Holy Spirit ask if I am willing to be a babushka. Am I ready to be a vessel the Lord longs to use in the lives of these children and grandchildren He intentionally placed in my life? Will I make the effort to fight for their salvation and protection? Will I rise early in the morning to pray fervently for them? In other words, am I willing to take up my prayer weapon and battle the Enemy for my family?

Why Another Teaching on Prayer?

Most grandparents have heard multiple sermons, Sunday school lessons, and studies on prayer. Why read another teaching on this subject? Since so much is at stake, learning all we can about prayer is critical. Prayer is one of the most powerful spiritual tools God has given to us. Yet prayer is probably the most underused tool we have. Due to the lies of the Enemy, the world, and our own minds, we fail to understand the power God has made available to us. If we realize the influence God has given to us, we can impact the eternal destiny of our loved ones, as well as their daily lives. We can become a life changer, making a difference in the generations following us. Therefore, it is worthwhile to examine once again this tool called prayer. Hopefully, these words will encourage and equip grandparents to fall to their knees and pray for their loved ones.

What Is Prayer?

Prayer is a conversation with God. It is coming into His mighty presence and talking to Him. Ruth Myers says, "Prayer is plugging into the almighty power of God."[9] As we approach God's throne in heaven, we know He is the supreme God. At our first breath, with our first words to Him, He is "inclining His ear" to us (Psalm 86:1, KJV). Through the redeeming blood of Jesus, we have the privilege of coming directly into our heavenly Father's throne room and of pouring out our hearts to Him. In Hebrews 4:14-16, we are told "to hold firmly to the faith that we profess" and "approach God's throne of grace with confidence, so that we may receive ... help ... in our time of need." Prayer is boldly

45

yet humbly coming before the Lord. It is opening our lives to Him so He, in His godly wisdom, can mold and shape our lives according to His purpose for us.

The A.C.T.S Prayer

How does a babushka approach prayer time? I confess at times I have struggled with this time of conversation with the Lord. One method I find compelling is the A.C.T.S. method. This acronym stands for Adoration, Confession, Thanksgiving, and Supplication. Sometimes I move quickly through these four levels of prayer. I pray only one or two sentences at each level, spending only a few minutes in prayer time. Other times, I move slowly and intentionally, basking in the presence of God. Occasionally, I linger at one level. Sometimes I get on my knees because there is something spiritually profound about physically humbling my body as I enter the presence of God. I imagine many Russian babushkas had tough-skinned knees from hours of prayer.

Appropriately, adoration is the first level of this prayer time. I turn my eyes on Jesus and use this time to focus on who God is. I meditate on the fact He *is* God. I do not use this time to ask for God's help for a loved one or for wisdom for a challenging situation. I do not thank Him for all He has done. Rather, I close my eyes and adore Him. Sometimes I sing a favorite hymn. How glad I am to be in a quiet corner away from people. Only the Lord hears my voice. And that is a good thing! But I know it blesses His heart to hear His daughter sing to Him.

Other times I read a few psalms. Some days I stand and read out loud a favorite psalm. Frequently, I turn to the beautiful Psalm 104. Or I love to recite Psalm 100. My third-grade

Sunday school teacher made sure each of her students learned that psalm. In my mind, I can still see this elderly woman with a big purple hat listening to her class recite the glorious words, "Make a joyful noise unto the Lord…" Amazingly, I have never forgotten that short but beautiful psalm. Many psalms direct me to get God's perspective on my life by channeling my attention to His presence surrounding me. My focus shifts from the world, my problems, and myself to the glorious reality of the Lord.

After reading a psalm or singing a hymn, I sit still for a few minutes, allowing the words I read or sang to saturate my heart. My thoughts become centered on God's awesomeness. "O, come let us adore Him…."

One Sunday morning, I was worshiping in church when I realized a profound fact. As I lift my voice in praise, I am joining the voices of "angels, archangels, and all the company of Heaven".[10] I gasped as I comprehended this glorious truth. I am uniting with all the company of heaven to worship and praise the Lord. I almost had to sit down. What a staggering honor to adore my King with all of His angels and archangels.

The beauty of these God-adoring moments is that I draw near to my loving Father. I am getting to know Him for who He is, growing in my relationship with my "Papa." I sing. I shout. Sometimes I whisper. By laying down my guard, I enjoy these moments of being in the sweet presence of the Lord. He loves it! Gradually, I do, too. When I take the time to adore the Lord, often I cannot wait until the next time I worship Him. Frequently, I hum the hymns throughout the day. I find the psalms rolling through my mind as I drive in my car or cook at the stove.

Next, I take time to confess before the Lord any sin that

comes to my mind. As I move from adoration to confession, I ask the Holy Spirit to show me my sins. Usually, I have to take a deep breath. Looking at the dark places of my life is uncomfortable. I ask the Lord to be gentle, to not give me too much to bear. "But please, Lord," I pray, "show me where I fail You." Sin is anything I say, do, or think that separates me from God. The list can be long. When I sin, I fall short of God's best for me, and I put distance between the Lord and me (Romans 3:23). Since God is holy and perfect, He cannot be a part of my sinfulness—hence, the gap between us. So I confess these sins. I say, "Lord, I know I have sinned by _____. I am sorry. Will you forgive me?" I give no excuses or explanations. I simply seek His forgiveness. Then I know He will be true to His Word and wash me as clean as snow (Isaiah 1:18).

Again, I sit still for a few minutes, letting these words sink into my spirit.

The third level of the A.C.T.S. prayer time is to thank the Lord for all the blessings in my life. There is so much for which to be thankful. Sometimes I give myself one minute to write down as many things as I can that the Lord has done for me or given to me. Next, I pray out loud over them, thanking Him for each one. This spiritual exercise helps me realize everything I have and all that I am comes from God. Without Him, I would have nothing. I would be nothing. Everything is a gift from my heavenly Father, who loves me more than I can imagine. First Corinthians 2:9 says, "No eye has seen, ... no ear has heard, ... no mind has conceived—the things God has prepared for those who love him." That's right. Neither you nor I can conceive all that God has prepared for us. If I sank to a low spot in my time of confession with the Lord, this third level of prayer time lifts my heart. I see how much the Lord has given me. I realize He loves me abundantly. What better way to spend a few minutes than to thank my Lord for His many gifts?

The fourth part of this prayer time is supplication. At this prayer level, grandparents make the most difference in the lives of their loved ones. During supplication, I talk to the Lord about the concerns and requests of my heart. I pray for loved ones who are struggling. I also seek God's guidance for challenging situations. Supplication prayer is placing my deepest concerns or heartaches at Jesus' feet. Standing in the gap for those I love, I intercede before heaven's throne on behalf of my family. I am honest and open about what keeps me awake at night. Some days I come to the Lord with a very heavy heart. I cry to Him, knowing He listens to every word and sees every tear. How awesome that the mighty God hears each of my concerns! Psalm 55:17 says, "Evening, morning and noon I cry out in distress, and he hears my voice."

One summer my three sons and my son-in-law each faced major decisions in their lives. My heart was heavy for these young men who were navigating the sometimes slippery and often steep paths of the twenty-first century. The importance of praying over my sons became evident to me. In my quiet time, I was reading Daniel. In the tenth chapter, I read about a great battle that continued for twenty-one days. I realized that praying once or twice was not enough to combat the battles my sons were facing. Similar to the man in Daniel 10, I prayerfully fought for twenty-one days on behalf of my sons. Out of that prayer time came jobs, mission trips, and, eventually, a beautiful daughter-in-law. There was nothing particularly spectacular about my prayers. For three weeks, I met the Lord early in the morning seeking His guidance for my sons. Occasionally, to this day, I pull out my *Twenty-One-Day Prayer Challenge*[11] to fight again on behalf of my sons.

God Answers Every Prayer

Not only does God hear every prayer but also He answers every prayer. Numerous Scriptures support this fact. Psalm 34:4 says, "I sought the Lord, and he answered me." "I call on you, my God, for you will answer me" is written in Psalm 17:6. Psalm 3:4 states, "I call out to the Lord, and he answers me from his holy mountain." Sometimes the Lord answers our requests with a "yes." Other times He answers with a "no." And occasionally, He answers them with "later." But He always answers His children's requests. In her book, *Praying God's Word Day by Day*, Beth Moore says, "Any 'no' an earnestly seeking child of God receives from the throne is for the sake of a greater 'yes.'"[12] Since God is always good, He knows what is best; His timing is perfect, and I am confident in His answer. I may not always like the answer. I may get impatient as I wait for His final answer. But I can always be at peace, assured that He is doing what is best.

God will not go against someone's will. For example, if you are praying for a wayward child, know God will not force anything on that child. He always allows that person a choice. God will work with the person. He will woo the person. But He will never force the person to make a certain choice. However, He may allow someone to become very miserable in his or her situation. But even then, the person has a choice. Psalm 145:8 says, "The Lord is gracious and compassionate, slow to anger and rich in love."

The Most Important Level of Prayer

Finally, there is a fifth level of prayer that does not appear in the A.C.T.S. acronym. However, I feel sure many babushkas live much of their prayer lives at this level. Perhaps this part of the prayer conversation is the most important piece. After completing the first four levels of prayer in which I have poured my heart through conversation with the Lord, I remain a few more minutes being still in God's presence. The fifth level of prayer conversation is waiting for and listening to God's words to me.

By definition, conversation is a two-way means of communication. It is not a lecture where only one person talks. So, when I have concluded conversing with the Lord, I linger for a few minutes. I become a "Rudy." The Lord patiently listens to my entire prayer conversation. But He longs for the opportunity to reply to me, to teach or direct my path. In Jeremiah 33:3 the Lord says, "Call to me and I will answer you and tell you great and unsearchable things you do not know." If I tarry in His presence and turn my ear to Him, He will tell me things I could not learn anywhere else. A babushka is intentional about carrying her concerns to the feet of Jesus. But she does not stop there. A babushka will remain in the Lord's presence. Sometimes she may sit for a few extra minutes. Other times she may linger for hours, waiting for the Lord to reveal His heartfelt answers.

Two Powerful Prayers

What does a babushka pray for her grandchildren? First and foremost, she prays for their salvation. In Ephesians, Paul gives us two examples of powerful prayers we can use for our loved ones who are seeking the Lord. These passages are also compelling when we're praying for someone searching for a deeper relationship with Christ. In Ephesians 1:15–19, Paul asks that the "eyes of [their] heart[s]" may be enlightened, or opened, to three things: one, the hope to which they have been called; two, the riches of their inheritance; and three, the "incomparably great power" available to those who believe. Whether I am praying for the salvation of a grandchild or for one seeking a deeper walk with the Lord, I prayerfully read these words from Ephesians. As I do, I know a dynamic prayer is being spoken over them. (See Appendix C: Prayer for the Salvation of a Grandchild.)

In Ephesians 3:16-19, Paul gives a second powerful prayer for those seeking the Lord or for those searching for a deeper relationship with Christ. Often I use this Scripture and insert the name of my grandchild in the verses. When I do, a mighty prayer evolves that is as applicable today as it was in Paul's time:

> *"I pray that out of His glorious riches God may strengthen Caleb with power through his Spirit in his inner being, so that Christ may dwell in his heart through faith. And I pray that he, being rooted and established in love, may have power, together with all the saints, to grasp how wide and long and high and deep is the love of Christ, and to know this love that surpasses knowledge—that he may be filled to the measure of all the fullness of God."*

The concluding verses of this third chapter, verses 20-21, give a powerful punch to end a prayer for any loved one:

"Now to him who is able to do immeasurably more than all we ask or imagine, according to his power that is at work within him, to him be glory in the church and in Christ Jesus throughout all generations, for ever and ever! Amen."

Since these words are from the Bible, I know I am praying powerful words. As I pray these Scriptures, I am confident my requests are in line with the heart of God. I know I am following a godly guideline that can potentially change the lives of my children and grandchildren forever. Their destiny is being divinely molded and shaped according to God's Word.

As a grandparent who desires to make a difference, I see the importance of praying for each person by name. Since I have thirteen children and grandchildren, I find it logistically necessary to pick one day a month to pray specifically for each person. Many days I will mention everyone. But on the day assigned to a particular person, I focus my prayers on him. Often I think through his needs on a physical, mental, spiritual, emotional, and psychological level. Then I lift these needs in prayer to the Lord during my time of supplication prayers.

Three Hindrances to Answered Prayer

At times I feel as if my prayers are not going any higher than the ceiling of the room. This reminds me that there are three great hindrances to answered prayer. The first one is unbelief. In Mark 11:24 Jesus tells me, "Whatever you ask for in prayer, believe that you have received it, and it will be yours." I must have faith in God that He will answer my prayer according to what He knows to be best.

The second hindrance is unforgiveness. In the next verse, Mark 11:25, Jesus says, "When you stand praying, if you hold anything against anyone, forgive him, so that your Father in heaven may forgive you your sins." When I hold judgment in my heart against anyone, the lines of communication with God are blocked.

The third hindrance is unconfessed sin. In 1 John 1:9 the aged, beloved disciple teaches, "If we confess our sins, he is faithful and just and will forgive us our sins and purify us from all unrighteousness." My prayer with God is obstructed when I hide sin in my heart. During my time of confession, I search my heart for anything that is displeasing to God—especially unbelief, unforgiveness, and unconfessed sin. In *Grandma, I Need Your Prayers*, authors Sherrer and Garlock say that once these are laid at the cross, the lines of communication with the Father are open. Then I can expect to receive an answer to my prayers.[13]

One More Reason

An additional reason to become a faithful, passionate prayer warrior is referenced in Revelation, the final book of the Bible. In chapter five, verses seven and eight, the elderly apostle John describes a heavenly scene where the twenty-four elders and living creatures fall down in deep worship before the Almighty God and His Son, the risen Jesus. The elders and living creatures bring only two items with them to worship: harps and golden bowls of incense. John explains the bowls of incense are the prayers of the saints.

Can you imagine? The prayers of God's people have been collected throughout human history and are offered as a gift of worship to the Father. In Revelation 8:3-5, John tells us an angel stands at the altar, holding much incense, in the presence of the omnipotent God. Again, John explains that the incense is the prayers of all the saints. He says, "The smoke of the incense, together with the prayers of the saints, went up before God." In Psalm 141:2, David also compares prayers to incense when he says, "May my prayer be set before you like incense."

As incense rises before God, so, too, do our fervent prayers. And as the incense is pleasing to God, so, too, do our prayers bring joy to our heavenly Father. Yes, each and every prayer that we grandparents utter, including the prayers we pray for our beloved children and grandchildren, is an invaluable treasure to our Lord God. Ponder the profoundness of this thought and let it grip your heart. You may feel as if your prayers are weak, faltering, simple. However, the next time you fall to your knees to pray for your loved ones, remember you are bringing a sweet fragrance to the Lord.

It is critical to pour our heartfelt prayer coverings over our families. It is an honor to bring joy to the heart of our heavenly Father.

Rising to the Occasion

The Lord placed my grandchildren in my life so I can become their babushka prayer warrior. He has given me the awesome opportunity to partner with Him on behalf of these dear ones. This is no accident. Nor is it incidental. Rather, it is intentional on His part. It is a part of His retirement plan for me. I can easily get caught in the busyness of life and push aside my prayer time. Yet it is one of the most important callings on my life as a grandparent.

As I age, I may become limited physically and that may make me feel useless. But even then, God has reasons for keeping me on earth. One potential reason is to prayerfully fight for my loved ones. Sometimes I may be the only person praying for them. My prayers can have eternal consequences on their lives. God knows the specific needs of each of my grandchildren. He longs to hear my babushka prayers on behalf of my loved ones.

Seizing this divine opportunity given to me by God, I become a life changer. This is grandparenting that makes a difference! Babushka prayers leave a legacy far more valuable than real estate or money. With urgency, I accept this calling to pray fervently for my grandchildren. I realize the hearts, minds, and lives of my grandchildren are at stake.

Will you join me as I rise—or should I say fall—to this occasion?

Key Three: Pray Fervently

"The prayer of a righteous person is powerful and effective."

JAMES 5:16

"As for me, far be it from me that I should sin against the Lord by failing to pray for you."

1 SAMUEL 12:23

"He hears the prayer of the righteous."

PROVERBS 15:29

Before they call I will answer; while they are still speaking I will hear.

ISAIAH 65:24

"Rejoice in the Lord always. I will say it again: Rejoice! Let your gentleness be evident to all. The Lord is near. Do not be anxious about anything, but in every situation, by prayer and petition, with thanksgiving, present your requests to God. And the peace of God, which transcends all understanding, will guard your hearts and your minds in Christ Jesus."

PHILIPPIANS 4:4-7

Study Questions

Chapter Four: Babushkas on Their Knees

Pounding It Out

1. What is a babushka? [A grandparent who prays fervently for her children and grandchildren] Why do you think Stalin thought he could take over Russia if he eliminated those "old women"? Explain why we need babushka-strong prayers today. See Ephesians 6:12.

2. What is prayer? [Conversation with God] How does a babushka approach prayer time? [Fervently, intentionally] Are you willing to be a babushka who daily fights through prayer for the salvation and protection of your loved ones?

3. What does the acronym A.C.T.S. represent? Which of these four levels of prayer time is the easiest for you? Which is the hardest?

4. Catherine spoke about a fifth level of prayer: waiting for God to speak and listening intently to what He says. Read Jeremiah 33:3. Why is it important for godly grandparents to tarry in God's presence?

5. What are the three hindrances to answered prayer? [Unbelief, unforgiveness, and unconfessed sin] Have you experienced one of these prayer obstacles? What can you do to remove these hindrances?

Driving It Home

1. Continue to be a Rudy and have a daily quiet time in God's Word this week. Remember to write down what speaks to you. Also, write down an action step to follow. (See The Three R's in chapter three.)

2. Add a period of quality prayer to your quiet time. Follow the A.C.T.S. guidelines. Tarry in God's presence as you conclude your babushka time. Remember, spending time in the Word and in prayer on behalf of your family are critical tools for becoming a godly grandparent.

RUNNING FOR LIFE

Key Four: Pursue Healthy Relationships

My youngest son, Jeff, is not a morning person. Some days he doesn't wake up before 10:00 a.m.—even though his body may have been upright for hours.

For years I drove Jeff to school every morning. There was no way he was going to make a 6:45 a.m. bus pickup. Some mornings there was little conversation in the car. But occasionally, he would perk up enough to talk to me. Over the years, I collected some special conversations in my heart. Today, I treasure the memory of those early morning rides with my sleepy son. All too soon, he got his driver's license and I was left at home.

Those few minutes between the school and our home

became a fertile ground in which the seeds of our mother-son relationship were planted. Of course, there were other nurturing grounds. But those car rides are memories I cherish.

The Reality of Relationships Today

In a culture crowded with smart phones, computers, and hectic schedules, relationships are often diminished—especially for grandparents. Living in a society that is ambiguous about our role, we grandparents struggle to develop deep ties with our families. As a result, many grandparents remain at a distance. Yet it is through meaningful relationships that hearts are connected and values, such as faith, are passed. Regardless of the depth of our faith, our spiritual impact on our families is greatly limited if we do not intentionally build healthy relationships with our loved ones. Strong heart ties with our children and grandchildren are the foundation of passing a legacy of faith in Jesus Christ to future generations.

We grandparents long to make a difference in the lives of our loved ones. We want to be life changers. But with many distractions and interferences, building strong ties within our families can be a challenge. As grandparents, we must become intentional in pursuing healthy relationships with our grandchildren. If we are not deliberate, even calculated, our legacy will be diminished or possibly demolished.

The fourth key in passing a legacy is the first key that includes our children or grandchildren. The previous three keys focused on preparing our hearts to impact the hearts of our loved ones. After surrendering our lives to the Lord (Key One), reading our Bibles every day (Key Two), and praying fervently like a babushka (Key Three), we are equipped to promote change in our family members.

To grasp the meaning of the fourth key, it is essential to comprehend the full definition of the word *pursue*. According to *Roget's 21ˢᵗ-Century Thesaurus*, "to pursue is to chase ... go after ... hunt down ... persevere, persist ... run down ... search out ..."[14] In other words, pursuing a healthy relationship with our loved ones is not a casual, laid-back, occasional effort. It is deliberately seeking, as often as feasible, the best possible relationship with our children and grandchildren. It is doing everything within our ability to maintain a solid connection with our loved ones.

Yes, I warmly remember riding in the car with Jeff. But that was a generation ago. Life is different now, but I still want to create similar moments with my grandchildren. I yearn for opportunities to connect my heart with theirs. However, I am often competing with modern technology for my grandchildren's attention. For many of us, our efforts are also complicated by distance and divorce. Therefore, we twenty-first-century grandparents need to become intentional about our relationships with our grandchildren.

What Is a Healthy Relationship?

First, we need to understand the difference between a healthy relationship and a loving relationship. Sometimes they are the same. That is the optimum. But in our turbulent times, many relationships are fragmented. This is particularly true when divorce is involved. Also, it can be difficult to maintain close ties when grandchildren live far away. Sometimes we must accept that the ideal is not an option. We may not always have the loving, warm relationship we desire. With diligent effort, however, it is possible in most situations to cultivate a healthy relationship.

There are several basic elements to a healthy relationship. First, respect is essential. Respect is treating our loved ones in thoughtful and courteous ways. We view their opinions, desires, and values as worthy of our serious consideration. We may not always agree with them, but we do earnestly regard their thoughts. It sounds simple, but often it takes diligent effort to treat each other in such a way. We may need to seek the Lord prayerfully to change our attitude toward a loved one, so we develop respect for that person. And we must give respect to receive it. Once respect is established, trust often follows.

A second factor in developing a strong relationship with our grandchildren is to have a healthy relationship with their parents, our grown children. If we do not have a viable relationship with their parents, it will be extremely difficult, if not impossible, to have a strong connection with our grandchildren. Before pursuing a meaningful relationship with our grandchildren, we should seek a healthy one with their parents. Invite your son or daughter over for a cup of coffee, or make time for a phone conversation where you explain your desire to be connected strongly to your grandchildren. Honesty is critical. If you have issues with your grown children, acknowledge them. When necessary and possible, seek forgiveness for past hurts. Be quick to offer your forgiveness for existing grievances. Mending these broken bridges is a vital part of a healthy relationship with the parents, as a well as with your grandchildren. We will look closely at repairing broken relationships in Chapter Six.

Third, having a healthy relationship does not mean we always agree or get along with our grandchildren. Most grandparents have concerns or issues with loved ones, especially as they grow older and life gets complicated. With respect as a base, however, we can honestly interact with our grandchildren. Even if we do not see eye to eye with a grandchild, we can pursue a meaningful relationship. Sometimes for the sake of the whole relationship, we must temporarily put aside the controversy by verbally acknowledging our differences. Be honest. Do not gloss over problems or pretend issues are not present. If it is helpful, set a time in the future to address these issues in a respectful way. Meanwhile, focus on the positive aspects of your relationship by inviting your grandchild to do something with you that you are sure he or she will enjoy.

The Importance of Healthy Relationships

The purpose of pursuing a strong relationship is to provide opportunities to tell your children and grandchildren frequently and assuredly that you love them unconditionally. Some grandparents are quick to express their love to their grandchildren. Others are less likely to say these words. Sometimes grandparents assume family members know they are loved, but that may not be true. Express your feelings often—face-to-face. My youngest grandson says, "I know you love me, Nina. You do not have to tell me." I reply, "Oh yes I do, Caleb! I never want you to forget how much your 'Nina' loves you."

As you communicate and demonstrate your love, you earn the right to tell them the most important message: God loves them and has a destiny for their lives. By expressing your love, you give your family a concrete example of parental love. This representation lays the foundation for them to understand and, hopefully, embrace the love and personal plans of their heavenly Father. The ultimate goal is for you to connect with their hearts so you can point them toward their heavenly Father's heart.

Ways to Build Healthy Relationships

Respect is one of the important factors in a healthy relationship. The first action step toward building such a relationship is to pray. Grab Key Three for passing a legacy. Become a babushka and pray fervently for your grandchild. Implore the Holy Spirit to empower you to develop a healthy relationship with this precious person He has placed in your life and under your care.

The next step is to spend time together. In a busy world where doing seems to be most important, just being with our grandchildren may be overlooked, minimized, or crowded out of our schedules. The most obvious way to be with our grandchildren is to spend time with them. Go to their house. Invite them to your home. When distance is a factor, schedule time together. Do this as often as possible.

Since the ultimate goal is to have a heart connection, provide an activity or atmosphere where you enjoy time together and engage in meaningful conversation. Arrange an activity that will lift your loved one's heart. Ice cream, milkshakes—maybe a cup of coffee if they are older—are easy ways to please a grandchild. The outing does not need to be expensive or time-consuming. Sometimes less is better.

It is tempting to fall into ruts when it comes to activities with our grandchildren. We may resort to TV or the movies since they are convenient options. But they do not effectively encourage meaningful conversation. Other choices will also delight your grandchild and provide excellent opportunities for heart-to-heart talks. But it takes time and creativity to discern places or activities that will be a treat for your loved one. Maybe your grandchild would enjoy one of the following:

- If they like music, go to a concert.
- Maybe they enjoy sports. Attend a game or watch one at home.
- Visit an art gallery.
- Paint or take a pottery class together.
- Go to a nearby park to hike or ride bikes through town.
- Do your grandchildren have an interest in architecture? Take a walk around your city and study the local buildings.
- Play miniature golf or go bowling, fishing, or hunting (with appropriate safety precautions).
- Have "Christmas in July" and work on some Christmas projects.
- Cook a favorite meal or bake a special treat together.
- Plant and tend to a garden with each other.

You get the idea. Do something to please the heart of your grandchild. Make it fun! Laugh! Kick up your heels and enjoy the moment. The goal is to be together.

A Word of Encouragement

Do not be disappointed if the time together does not go as planned. Often I have to improvise. Recently, I found a great

Lego activity online, or so I thought. I was excited to try it with my grandkids. However, within a few minutes of introducing the game, I found myself sitting at the kitchen table alone because the kids had slipped quietly outside to swing in the hammock. I left the Legos and joined them. We talked and had fun. Things do not always go the way we plan. But trust the Lord to use the time together as He sees best.

The Most Important Moment

Most crucial of all, at some point in the outing, specifically tell your grandchildren you love them, respect them, and are proud of them. Use your own words, but express your heart for each one. It does not have to be a lengthy conversation. Start by telling them they are special. They are precious. They are unique. In fact, Ephesians 2:10 says they are God's masterpiece. You love them because God loved them first and placed them in your life. (See Appendix B for suggestions on starting conversations.)

If it is uncomfortable to speak such words, close the conversation. But if it is going well, continue. Point out your grandchild's strengths, giftedness, and uniqueness. Affirm his or her value. Make this clear: "I love you for who you are, not for what you do." Explain that God created them in His image with a plan for their lives. He gave them strengths and weaknesses to point them in His designed direction. As you share these powerful words, you develop a sense of destiny within them. This gives them biblical vision, hope, and excitement for living the life God created for them.

Other Ways to Connect

While time together is the best and easiest way to build healthy relationships, sometimes I use other options to connect:

- **Regular Phone Calls.** I love to pick up the phone and call my grandchildren. Even though they may not always be available for conversation, I have found phone calls to be great connection points. I pray before I call. I ponder what I know to be going on in their lives presently. Then I have questions to ask them about their day or other events. On occasion, I simply call to chat, letting them know I am thinking about them and I wanted to say "hi." The conversation does not need to be long. Even a short call is a statement of love. Of course, face time is an even stronger means of connecting.

- **Snail Mail.** Young or old, everyone loves to get a letter in the mail. The note does not need to be long. One page is fine. The point is to connect in a loving, supportive way. Also, I find Hallmark cards a great means to say, "You are special to me." Always I sign the letter or card, "I love you, Nina." We will study more closely in Chapter Seven ways to leave written legacies to grandchildren.

- **Modern Means of Communication.** When coupled with more traditional approaches, modern means of communication add to strong relationships. Typical of their generations, my children and grandchildren respond well to texting. Emailing is a distant second but still worth the effort in certain situations. If you do not know how to text, make the effort to learn. It is an easy, quick, and direct means to your grandchildren once they have a phone. Emailing allows for longer, more specific messages.

Regardless of where or how you spend time with your grandchild, include words that express how much you love them. Remember these words are the most important ones to use during your time together.

Lay the Foundation for Your Date

Before you go on your date with your loved one, let them know your desire is to treat them. When I began intentionally to develop strong relationships with my grown children, my oldest son, Chris, was perplexed.

We were sitting in a small ice cream parlor near his college apartment. Since he was under so much pressure to complete his Master's degree, I visited him, hoping to shower him with some motherly love. But when I started a serious conversation, he questioned me. "What are you up to? Why are you being so attentive?"

"I love you, Chris. Now that you're an adult, I want to pursue the best possible relationship with you."

He eyed me cautiously over the top of his ice cream cone, but he relaxed as I assured him my intention was to do something special simply because I loved him. "God has placed you in my life for a reason, and I want to live into that reason. I'm so thankful that you're my son."

That day I learned it is important for my loved one to understand my intention. Otherwise, he may feel manipulated or controlled rather than loved. I adored my dark-haired, sweet-spirited son when he was a little boy. Now I want to love him as an adult—which may require different approaches and attitudes—but it is vital for him to know that my love for him remains the same.

Perhaps your life has been busy for the past several weeks, months, or even years. Clarify to your loved one that you recognize your preoccupation but desire to draw close to them now. Maybe needs from other family members have dominated your time. Now you desire to connect with them. Or maybe you simply did not know to be intentional about a close relationship with your children or grandchildren. You have learned this key and yearn to put it into practice.

When Distance Is a Factor

If your grandchildren live too far away to spend an afternoon or evening together, make a date with them. Have a conversation over the phone similar to one of those I described above. Maybe you could add an interesting twist by suggesting that both of you go to your local Starbucks or a special restaurant that is in both places. Skype or FaceTime with each other so you can still talk face-to-face. Be sure to tell them you love them.

Important Characteristics of a Godly Grandparent

Godly grandparents have many significant qualities. These four are of top importance:

- **Authenticity.** I hope you can tell your grandchildren "I love you" easily and often. That is a significant and meaningful part of many healthy relationships. But it is also important to be authentic with your grandchildren. If you cannot genuinely say "I love you" then do not say it. You can use other sincere, affirming statements. Tell them you are trying to be the best grandparent you can be. Explain that they are important to you. Tell them you care deeply about them. None of those, however, are quite the same as saying those three simple but profound words, "I love you." But honesty is essential. Young people can sense when you are not being true. Unauthentic statements, even when they come from a loving heart, can seriously undermine a healthy relationship.

- **Integrity.** Be a person of integrity. The *Merriam-Webster Dictionary* defines *integrity* as "the quality or state of being complete or undivided."[15] A person of integrity is one who lives his life firmly committed to what is right, true, and noble. Such a person does not waver even in the small things. By striving to be this person, you are modeling Christlike principles. For such virtue, you will be respected and loved even in situations where differences may exist. Integrity goes a long way to providing the environment for a healthy, meaningful relationship.

- **Faithfulness.** Be a person of faithfulness who is committed to know, love, and serve Jesus Christ all the days of your life. Implement the first three keys for passing a legacy: surrender to Christ, read the Bible daily, pray fervently. These keys prepare you to connect on a heart level with your grandchild.

* **Honor.** Finally, be a grandparent who honors his or her loved ones. This word is grossly misunderstood in our culture. Living in the Western world where self-gratification abounds, honoring your grandchild may be considered unnecessary, perhaps even inappropriate. Scott Turansky and Joanne Miller of the National Center for Biblical Parenting state, "To honor someone is to treat them as special, to do more than is expected and to do it with a good attitude."[16] Honor is more than a certain behavior. It is a selfless perspective, which originates in the heart. When grandparents honor their loved ones, they open the door for a heart connection that ultimately leads to sharing the love of Christ.

Life Changers

Yes, pursuing healthy relationships with our grandchildren takes time, effort, and creativity. This is true whether we are face-to-face or far away. Due to the demands of the twenty-first century, grandparents need to be diligent in cultivating healthy relationships. If we are serious about being a life changer to our loved ones, we must become intentional. Remember, hearts are connected and values are passed through meaningful relationships. Regardless of our faith, our impact on our grandchildren is limited if we do not run after a healthy relationship. Our mission as godly grandparents is to communicate three things to our loved ones: 1) our unconditional love for them, 2) God's unconditional love for them, and 3) that God has a plan for them.

The big picture of life as God intended is for families across the generations to do life together. Too often, though, we get caught in the busyness of our routine. We forget God's design. His discipleship plan for grandparents, as well as parents, has always been to develop a heart connection with each family member. By connecting to our loved ones' hearts, we are positioned to connect them with their Abba Father. We can strengthen that connection with encouragement for each person to know, love, and serve the Lord. Then one day we will spend eternity together.

The morning car rides with my son Jeff occurred two decades ago. Times were different. As you pick up Key Four for passing a legacy, know you are investing in the next generation of your family. Not only are you impacting the life of your daughter or granddaughter, son or grandson, but also you are investing in future generations. By pursuing healthy relationships, you are planting seeds that will bear fruit for generations to come. You are a life changer, influencing not only your generation but also the generations that follow. You are a grandparent making a difference.

Key Four: Pursue Healthy Relationships

"Tell it to your children, and let your children tell it to their children and their children to the next generation."

JOEL 1:3

"Love must be sincere. Hate what is evil; cling to what is good. Be devoted to one another in brotherly love. Honor one another above yourselves. Never be lacking in zeal, but keep your spiritual fervor, serving the Lord."

ROMANS 12:9-11

Study Questions

Chapter Five: Running for Life

Pounding It Out

1. How are values, such as faith, passed from one person to another? [Through relationships] If you are strong in your faith but do not have a healthy relationship with your grandchildren, how realistic is it that you can pass a legacy of faith in Christ to them?

2. What does it mean to have a healthy relationship with your children and grandchildren? If you disagree with them or get angry at them, does that mean you are not in a healthy relationship with them? [Not at all. In fact, it is healthy to be honest about your thoughts or feelings. Few people in close relationships avoid disagreements. The key in such situations is to respond thoughtfully rather than react emotionally.]

3. Brainstorm ways to spend quality time with your grandchildren.

4. How does Catherine suggest you invite your grandchild to spend time together if there are issues between the two of you? [Admit you have differences, but explain that, for this occasion, you want to put these issues aside and spend time together. In establishing healthy relationships, it is important to be honest and authentic.]

5. What is the goal of this time together? [To tell your grandchild three things: 1) you love them unconditionally, 2) God loves them unconditionally, and 3) God has a plan for their lives.]

Driving It Home

1. Have Rudy time several times this week. Remember the urgent calling of the Lord for you to lift up babushka-strong prayers for your loved ones.
2. Do something this week to connect with at least one of your children or grandchildren.

   a. Go out for a cup of coffee or light meal. Ask questions like these:

   > How are you doing?
   > What is going well in your life?
   > What is challenging for you?
   > Can I be of help? How?
   > If possible, say, "I love you for who you are, not for what you do."

   b. If getting together is not possible, then call your loved one on the phone. Use the questions above.
   c. Email or text the above questions to your loved ones.
   d. Write a short letter or send a Hallmark card to say, "I love you!"
   e. In your babushka prayer time, pray for the Lord to help you establish good relationships with your loved ones.

The purpose of this time together is to develop relationships by affirming and encouraging your loved one. See Appendix B for Conversation Starters.

Is There a Doctor
in the House?

Key Five: Heal Broken Relationships

We live in a fractured and sinful world. The Bible tells us in Romans 3:23, "All have sinned and fall short of the glory of God." One result of sin is many grandparents have broken relationships with their grown children or grandchildren. Some have serious issues while others have less critical concerns. Certain problems are blatantly obvious; other contentions are subtle. Some grandparents deal with the heartbreaking reality of grandchildren who have rebelled, left home, and have not been seen for months or even years. Other grandparents have concerns about a grandchild's academic grades, activities, or friends. But we all probably have a strained relationship on some level with at least one family member. Healing these broken relationships is vital if you desire to impact the heart of your loved one for Christ.

Due to the brokenness within their families, many grandparents have heavy hearts. They may have struggled for years, decades, or even a lifetime with the hurt, pain, and emotional distance from family members they love deeply. When I lead workshops, a grandparent will often ask if there is hope for loving family relationships that are riddled with deep brokenness. Convinced hurtful relationships are unredeemable, these grandparents feel hopeless. They may be resigned to a distant relationship or no relationship at all.

By the grace and power of God, there is always hope!

Our sinfulness is never too egregious for the Lord to redeem. In fact, the redemption of all sin, of which brokenness is a part, is the desire of God's heart. That is why He sent His only Son, Jesus, to the cross. Through the shed blood of Jesus, we forever have hope for redeemed relationships with our children and grandchildren.

Different Issues Require Different Solutions

You cannot handle all problems the same way. Some situations require counseling. Professional wisdom can be God's wisdom. However, there are three powerful steps each of us can take to move toward a healthier relationship with our estranged loved ones. The result may not be the rosy, intimate relationship we desire. But by following these steps, we can improve our relationships. The Enemy wants us to think these issues are permanent. We readily believe his evil lie because the pain, anger, and bitterness are great. The proverbial elephant in the room seems unmovable.

But our God is a mighty God. He desires that our family relationships be whole and healthy more than we do. In Isaiah 61:1, the Bible says the Messiah, whom we know is Jesus, is coming to heal the brokenhearted. Definitely included in God's redemption plan are grandparents with broken family relationships. First, we must get our loved ones' attention. More importantly, we must reach their hearts so we can point them to Christ.

Mending Broken Relationships Is a Process

Mending relationships requires time, humility, and effort. Seldom is there a quick fix. Healing is not a drive-through, quick-action solution that our culture often expects. If the brokenness runs deep, the redemption will take time.

My experience with brokenness taught me that to mend a relationship I need to diligently pursue the Lord. For months, this relationship was a top priority in my life. Also, I needed babushka-strong prayers since I could not repair this broken relationship without the Lord. I relied on the Holy Spirit to go before me and to clear a path for me to follow. I became sensitive to His leading rather than attempting to resolve the issues on my own.

A Grandparent's God-Given Influence

In chapter one, we discussed God's desire for parents and grandparents to have a powerful, positive influence on the hearts and minds of their loved ones. This power is unparalleled. Our words have the potential to reach far beyond the words of anyone else. Contrary to prevailing Western cultural beliefs, this biblical truth is a reality for every child or grandchild. It does not matter if your loved one is three years old or thirty years old. If there is breath in you and in them, you have a God-given power to reach their hearts. The method of impacting their hearts changes as they age. But the power remains until one of you goes to heaven.

The Crux of the Matter

Simply stated, the crux of mending a broken relationship is connecting with the heart of your alienated loved one. When hurtful issues exist between two people, understand that the wounded person has built a wall of protection around his heart. Your loved one has distanced himself from you to keep his heart safe from further pain. Your beloved may be intentional about the separation; sometimes, however, the wall is erected on a subconscious level. If there is unresolved hurt between you and him, he considers you a danger. Consequently, this loved one detaches from you. Satan wants that disconnection to remain. When possible, he will widen it. By doing so, this compelling enemy puts the heart of your loved one in bondage.

Remember, though, faith is passed through a heart connection. The greatest legacy you give your children and grandchildren is a relationship with Jesus Christ. Our divinely assigned task is to guide all our family members toward God—to know Him intimately, love Him passionately, and serve Him faithfully. By keeping your loved one in bondage over an issue, Satan steals that person's relationship with you, as well as with his heavenly Father. The stakes are high. Your loved one's eternal destiny may be at risk.

Biblical Steps to Mending Broken Relationships

Several years ago, Dr. Rob Rienow of Visionary Family Ministry wrote a profound book, *Never Too Late*, to encourage parents whose grown children have walked away from their faith in Christ. I devoured the book, looking for ways to bring all my children into a personal relationship with the Lord. Rienow teaches four biblical principles, which provide practical steps to reach the hearts of your loved ones. This chapter is heavily based on Rienow's first three steps.[17] Chapter eight of this book is devoted entirely to his fourth step—pointing the heart of your loved one toward the Lord. In this current chapter, I only skim the surface of his discussion on the first three principles. If broken relationships are an issue for you, I strongly encourage you to read his book or watch his DVD, *Never Too Late*, which is based on the book. You can go to visionaryfam.com for more information.

Today, I am blessed to have loving relationships with my children and grandchildren. We are not perfect. Our relationships are not always wonderful. At times, I have definitely relied on the principles of Rienow's book. Presently, our family has healthy relationships with each other most of the time; however, I cannot say the same about my relationship with my husband. Several years ago, he divorced me after seven years of struggling to save our marriage of thirty-four years.

The failure grieved me, but Rienow's biblical steps of reconciliation gave me hope and direction in my relationships with my hurting children, as well as with my estranged husband. I share them with you out of my own brokenness, assured of God's grace and redemption in very dark places.

Step One: Turn Your Heart to the Lord

As explained in Chapter Two, the first key of godly grandparenting is to surrender your heart to the Lord. In reconciling broken relationships with your grandchildren or children, the crucial starting point is looking first at your relationship with Jesus Christ.

When I am seeking redemption of a broken or strained relationship, I ask the Lord to show me any barriers that exist between Him and me. I become like Rudy, drawing near to my Lord and Savior. Hebrews 12:1 says, "Let us throw off *everything* that hinders and the sin that so easily entangles, and let us *run* with perseverance the race marked out for us" (emphasis added). Remembering that sin is anything I say, do, or think, which separates me from God, I put on my babushka mantle. I fervently pray for the Holy Spirit to show me the sin in my life. Like Rudy, I sit close to my Master, drawing from His wisdom and love. I ask Him to show me where there is brokenness between us. I talk to Him about these revelations and tell Him I am sorry. I pause. I ask for His forgiveness. I have learned that if I desire to be reunited with my loved one, then I must first be united with the Lord.

Nothing we have ever said, done, or thought is too much for the Lord to forgive. If we are genuinely remorseful, then He has promised to forgive us. Our relationship is restored. Sometimes guilt lingers. But that is from our Enemy, who will attempt on every level to keep us separate from God. We need to recognize the lie and replace it with God's truth. We are forgiven if we are sorry and confess our sin to Him (1 John 1:9).

Do not rush through this first step. Take your time. Linger in the presence of the Lord. Open your ears to hear His words. Then be obedient to what He tells you. A hurried start will challenge, if not compromise, your entire effort to mend your broken relationship with your child or grandchild. Sometimes it may take days or weeks of dwelling on Step One for your relationship with the Lord to be restored. Remember, mending broken relationships is a process. It takes time for the Holy Spirit to prepare your heart for the upcoming steps.

Summary for Step One: Repentance before the Lord

Step Two: Turn Your Heart to Your Child
Once I feel led by the Holy Spirit to move to the second step, I go to a quiet place to spend time with my Lord. I search my heart and memory for anything I may be holding against my grown child or grandchild. I ask myself several questions: When he was young, did he embarrass me? Has he hurt my feelings? Did he say or do something to anger me, which created the distance between us? Are recent issues causing separation between us? Have I compassionately discussed these issues with my beloved?

A simple example might be when your teenager was learning to drive. One day, he accidentally damaged your car. Your insurance increased, which cost you several thousands of dollars over time. Do you feel today that he "owes" you that money? Have you confessed your feelings to the Lord? Have you told your child you forgive him?

85

Your situation might have much deeper roots. Your child or grandchild may have betrayed you, rebelled against you, or run away. For years, maybe you did not know where your child was living. That may have hurt you deeply. Be honest with the Lord and with yourself. Do not minimize these heart issues. They are real feelings that need to be addressed. Seek your loving Father who understands every thought or feeling. Implore Him to give you compassion for the child who has hurt you.

After I search my heart, I go to the Lord in babushka prayer time, asking Him to show me any anger or resentment within me toward my beloved. Sometimes these hurtful, embarrassing, or uncomfortable memories have been buried in the far recesses of my heart. It seems easier to leave the bad memories alone. I tell myself I have forgotten those offenses, or I say they do not matter anymore. But distance has developed between my loved one and me. If not confessed and forgiven, the brokenness will continue to exist.

Next, I ask the Lord to give me the grace and power of the Holy Spirit to forgive my child. "Help me let the issue go," I pray. "Help me to lay it down at the foot of the cross." When I release the situation to the Lord, He is responsible to handle it—not me. I specifically ask for compassion for my loved one. I pray, "Help me, Lord, to understand him that I may forgive him."

Remember that forgiveness is not condoning someone's behavior or actions. Forgiveness releases you from the bondage of the broken situation. Also keep in mind that forgiveness is not based on your feelings toward this person. Instead, forgiveness is a step of faith you take—that is, through the grace and power of the Holy Spirit, you release this person to the Lord. Often your feelings of forgiveness come later in the process.

After I release the situation to the Lord, I go to my loved one. I tell him I forgive him for this grievance. If it has been years since the offense occurred, I ask him if he remembers when it happened. Then I ask him to forgive me for holding this grudge against him.

As in Step One, do not hurry through Step Two. Take the required time to search your heart and mind for any grievances you may be harboring toward your child or grandchild. Give the Lord ample time to minister to you on this level. We are accustomed to immediate results, but God does not always act according to our schedule. At times, He desires for us to percolate in a situation. Those extra moments spent in His presence or in conversation with our loved one can deliver a deeper redemption that sets the foundation for a strong, healthy relationship at the end. Enjoy these moments with the Lord and with your child or grandchild. Allow your heart to be filled with love and compassion for this special person God placed in your life. Savor the time of building stronger connections. They are worthy of the invested time.

Summary for Step Two: Compassion Leading to Forgiveness

Consider Your Child's Perspective

God intends for grandchildren to enjoy a loving relationship with their grandparents. These "grand" people appointed by the Lord are intended to point their loved one's heart toward Him. But issues arise. Sin enters. Brokenness happens and loved ones withdraw. Sometimes the withdrawal is obvious—a physical one. Your family member may refuse to hug you or to speak to you. Perhaps he refuses to be in your presence. Other times, the separation is subtle—an emotional withdrawal. This withdrawal can be lethal because you cannot see it. Your loved one may act as if everything is fine. But in his heart, your loved one has an issue. He has built a wall around his heart. There is brokenness between the two of you. He may engage you, talk to you. But in his heart, he has distanced himself from you. He wears a mask that bears a smile. Behind the mask, however, his face is sad or angry. Your loved one has locked his heart. To reach his heart for the Lord is impossible at this point. Step Three is to clear the relationship between you and your loved one from his perspective so you may point his heart toward the Lord.

Step Three: Draw Your Child's Heart to Your Heart
In your Rudy time with the Lord, ask the Holy Spirit to show you where you have hurt or disappointed your loved one. Tarry in God's presence. Wait for Him to reveal to you the anger and bitterness that resides in your loved one. You may have to go to the Lord numerous times before you get the complete picture of the situation.

Prayerfully and carefully, go to your grown child or grandchild. Ask him if there is anything over the years you have done to offend him.

Ask him for his forgiveness for what the Holy Spirit revealed to you.

Ask him for his forgiveness for what he admitted to you.

There are four critical steps in seeking forgiveness:

1. Confess your part.
2. Say, "I was wrong." Resist the urge to explain your actions.
3. Ask, "Will you forgive me?" These words are essential.
4. Once your loved one can look you in the eyes and confess,

    "I forgive you," ask if he will give back his heart to you. During this time of brokenness, he has withheld his heart from you. Ask if he will trust you again with his heart. Your desire is for an open, honest, intimate relationship again.

    Tell him, "This is important to me, my grandson."
5. If your loved one hesitates to forgive you, tell him that you want to give him time to consider your request for forgiveness. He may forgive you, or he may not. It is his choice. Sometimes it takes time for a person to make this decision. You do not want to force the issue or pressure him into saying he forgives you. You are seeking authentic and complete forgiveness. Come back in a few days or a week. Ask again for his forgiveness. You may need to address the issue multiple times. Sometimes it takes days, weeks, even years for his heart to be softened to the point of true forgiveness. But it is important for him to say, "I forgive you." Do not accept "it's okay" or "don't worry about it, Grandma."

Remember, these steps do not fix a problem. If correction is needed, tell your loved one you will have a conversation at another time to discuss necessary disciplinary action. The focus of this conversation is forgiveness. Also, any explanation of your actions should be given at another time. In this conversation, you simply confess your wrongdoing. Be careful not to make excuses, which can easily undermine your confession and risk the loss of his forgiveness. Your goal is to receive your loved one's genuine forgiveness. These steps, if carried to completion, can open the doors to a healthy and honest relationship. Sometimes it takes repeated encounters to reach full forgiveness. This is heart-work. It may take time. Once you receive authentic forgiveness, you can move toward healing your broken relationship.

Summary for Step Three: Confession to Your Loved One

Building New Foundations

If you had a broken relationship with a loved one, you will want to intentionally build a new foundation for that relationship. Here are a few guidelines for establishing a healthy connection:[18]

1. Tell your adult child you want to always have an open, honest relationship with him. Admit you may not always agree on everything, but you want to strive for authenticity.
2. This may be awkward for you. Uncomfortable. Admit that to your child.
3. State that you always want his honesty—even if what he has to say is hard to hear. If he does say something hard to hear, simply say that you appreciate his honesty and that you hear him.
4. Focus on speaking with extra respect to your sons and with extra gentleness to your daughters. Sons thrive

and respond to respect from their parents—especially from dads. Use a respectful tone of voice. God built the feminine heart to respond to love and gentleness. God created women in such a way that they respond with warmth, love, and closeness when someone treats them with gentleness and love.

5. Seek to understand before seeking to be understood. A running theme with young people is "My parents don't understand me. They're constantly trying to lecture me, fix me, and change me." The result is your adult child is increasingly becoming resistant to your relationship and will often try to avoid you.

6. If you want to draw your child's heart to you and rebuild the heart connection, you must commit yourself to giving maximum effort to understanding your son or daughter, not just seeking to be understood by him or her. We need to commit to listening to our children before our children can open their hearts to receive our words and influence.

7. In your quiet time with God, ask for His grace and power to help you learn from, listen to, and understand your adult child.

Burned Hands

In closing, I will share a story that is dear to my heart. Hopefully, it will concretely illustrate to you the steps of mending a broken relationship.

Ella, my seven-year-old granddaughter, went to her neighborhood school playground to have some fun. Inside the school library, her mom—my daughter, Carrie—was painting a mural. It was a sweltering August day for the Charleston area with temperatures hovering above 100 degrees. In that extreme heat, Ella jumped onto metal monkey bars. They were blazingly hot. To her horror, the bars burned her hands. The next few hours were scary. Carrie took Ella to the ER. Ella's pink skin turned ashen as blisters appeared. Anxiously watching her daughter, Carrie wondered about the prognosis of these precious hands.

The ER doctors did what they do so well. They cared for this frightened mother and wounded daughter with compassion and gentleness. They cut away the dead skin on Ella's hands, applied burn ointments, and then wrapped her small hands in gauze. Specific instructions were given for home care before Carrie and Ella headed out the door.

Today, I am grateful that my little Ella's hands are healed. With each passing day the pain subsided. Eventually, healthy skin replaced the burned wounds. Isn't it amazing that hands with second-degree burns can become healthy hands again? Personally, I marvel at the genius of our Creator God.

Broken relationships are similar to burned hands. Perhaps you or your loved one has been "burned." You have experienced painful situations with this person, which have caused various levels of hurt, anger, or fear. But the Lord God is fully capable of healing wounded relationships. It may take time for the hurt to drain, the anger to subside, and the fear of relationship with this person to be removed. It may be an uphill battle. When I face such a challenging situation, I always ask myself, "Is this person worth the investment of my time or energy? Is he worth opening my heart to a painful relationship again?"

Where family members are concerned, the answer is a resounding "Yes!" It is never too late, and it is never too difficult for the Lord to bring a parent/child or a grandparent/grandchild into a close relationship. Again, it may not be the ideal situation. Each person chooses to pursue a healthy relationship or to remain distant. But any improvement is worth the risk, right? Maybe one small step will lead to another small step. Like burned skin, broken relationships heal slowly. And in both cases, the healing starts on the inside and works outward. One layer must heal before the next one.

The Enemy wants us to believe our situation is hopeless. He convinces us it can never be anything more than it is presently. To battle him, I encourage you to be a Rudy. Run to the Lord and seek His face on behalf of this loved one. Fall on your knees as a praying babushka and fervently ask your heavenly Father to show you His way to reach the heart of your loved one. You do not have to accept the brokenness. It will take work, patience, and perseverance to step out of your comfort zone and mend this precious relationship with your loved one.

You Are Not Alone

Know that the Lord is with you every step of the way. It is fully the desire of His heart for you to mend the broken relationships with your loved ones. By His grace and power, He will equip you to be a life changer by reaching the hearts of your children and grandchildren. If you ask Him, He will go before you. He will walk alongside you. He will be behind you, protecting you in every way. Our God is a mighty God. When the healing is complete, not only has the relationship between an earthly parent or grandparent and his loved one been redeemed, but also the relationship between the heavenly Father and His child has been preserved. It is worth the time, effort, and risk to mend broken relationships. Your loved one can be set free from hurt, pain, anger, and bitterness that have been plaguing him for years. He is positioned for the beginning of an eternal relationship.

Key Five: Heal Broken Relationships

"The Spirit of the Sovereign Lord is on me, because the Lord has anointed me to preach good news to the poor. He has sent me to bind up the brokenhearted, to proclaim freedom for the captives and release from darkness for the prisoners."

ISAIAH 61:1

"To him who is able to keep you from falling and to present you before his glorious presence without fault and with great joy—to the only God our Savior be glory, majesty, power and authority, through Jesus Christ our Lord, before all ages, now and forevermore! Amen."

JUDE 24

Study Questions

Chapter Six: Is There a Doctor in the House?

Pounding It Out

1. Romans 3:23 says "all have sinned and fall short of glory of God." One common result of our sin is that we have issues with our loved ones. The Enemy wants us to think these issues are hopeless. Read Isaiah 61:1. Is there hope? Why?

2. It is important to realize three facts about healing broken relationships:

   a. Healing broken relationships is a process, not a to-do list.

   b. This process takes time. It is not a quick fix. Healing relationships requires an investment of time and an establishment of priorities.

   c. Healing broken relationships takes much prayer empowered by Holy Spirit.

   Which of these three facts is challenging to you? Which is easiest for you to accept?

3. The first step in healing broken relationships is to turn your heart to the Lord. This means to clear the relationship between the Lord and you. What are the barriers that cause distance or brokenness in your relationship with the Lord? What is the Summary Phrase for Step One? [Repentance before the Lord]

4. Who is walking with you in this adventure of mending broken relationships? [The Lord and other godly grandparents seeking to impact the lives of their loved ones].

5. Much is at stake in mending broken relationships. Do you believe the time, effort, and risk is worth the effort? Why or why not?

Driving It Home

1. Have Rudy time and babushka time daily.

2. The second step in healing a broken relationship is to turn your heart toward your child. Focus on your heart first. Make a list of the issues you are holding against your child. How long have you been harboring these issues? Pray to release these grievances. Tell your child that you forgive him or her. What is the Summary Phrase for Step Two? [Compassion leading to forgiveness]

3. Step Three in healing a broken relationship is to draw your child's heart to your heart.

   a. Clear the relationship between your child and you by focusing on their heart. Ask yourself, "What have I done to them to cause distance or brokenness between us?" Can you tell your child where you were wrong in this situation? [Note: You are confessing your wrong part. You are not confessing or condoning any wrong behavior on the part of anyone else].

b. Can you ask your loved one to forgive you for your part? What do you do if he or she hesitates to forgive you? [Tell your loved one to take time and ponder your confession. You can discuss the situation again at a later date. It is important for your loved one's forgiveness to be authentic]. Why is authentic, full forgiveness important?

c. What is the Summary Phrase for this third step? [Confession to your loved one]

4. In the section titled Building New Foundations, Catherine stated that sons respond well to respect. To what do daughters respond well? List two ways to show respect to your sons and grandsons. List two ways to show love and gentleness to your daughters and granddaughters.

CHAPTER SEVEN

PENCILS, NOTEBOOKS, AND COMPUTERS

Key Six: Leave a Written Legacy of Love

"If you were to die today, what would your children hold in their hands tomorrow that would let them know they were the treasures of your life?"[19]

I will be honest. I am a pack rat. I save everything, especially pieces of paper. Sometimes I feel like I am watching a rerun of my mother's life. In my childhood home, near our kitchen phone (remember those?), the counter overflowed with papers. In Mama's bedroom, her desk was covered with various notes, letters, and who-knows-what. She knew exactly what was in each pile. Her unspoken rule was "don't touch anything on my desk."

Many years later, I helped Mama clean out her attic because she was moving to a condo. Since she had lived in her home for over thirty years, clearing the attic was an enormous job. One day I found some letters in an old shoebox. "Mama," I said, "look at these letters!"

Her eyes sparkled as she explained, "Those are some letters my mother wrote me when I was in college. She wrote one every Sunday afternoon."

My grandmother's commitment to write my mother amazed me. I then remembered that my mother had telephoned me every Sunday afternoon when I was in college. Then I realized how few letters I had written to my children when they were in college. Email had been our main communication tool.

Modern technology has made my life easier and even more enjoyable. I delight in using FaceTime to connect with my long-distance family. Texting is quick and easy, especially when I can include all four of my children in a group text. Last week, I communicated with my grandson *while* he was touring at Disneyworld. My family is always within reach because my phone is by my side 24/7. Yes, twenty-first-century communication has many advantages.

But it comes with some serious disadvantages, too. With technology infiltrating our world, the written word is declining. Nevertheless, by writing messages, personal stories, and blessings to our loved ones, grandparents can significantly impact their loved ones' lives.

A Written Legacy of Love

The sixth key for passing a legacy of faith to our children and grandchildren is to leave a written legacy of love. Yes, it's easy to pick up the phone and call someone, and FaceTime brings us directly into the room with our faraway grandchildren. But once the call has ended or the FaceTime is complete, there is no paper trail. Our conversations about events and our expressions of love are lost to cyberspace. They may be tucked away in our hearts, but eventually memories will fade. Those weekly letters from my grandmother to my mom were a written record of her family farm life in the 1930s. More importantly, the letters were a printed testimony of love and blessing inscribed from one generation to the next.

Why Is a Written Legacy Important?

Writing letters, stories, or blessings to our loved ones is important for many reasons. First, written messages affirm and encourage our children and grandchildren. When we write a note to our family members, we often write messages we may think or feel but seldom say. Sometimes it is easier to write an intimate thought than to speak it, so it is vital to communicate and record these messages for the next generation. Writing messages gives us the opportunity to record those three most significant words, "I love you." As I mentioned in Chapter Five, hopefully, you can say these words to your loved ones. But writing these words is also extremely valuable. Even though we may demonstrate our love in numerous ways, it is critical to say *and* write them to our children and grandchildren.

Second, leaving a written legacy preserves family stories. Our written accounts of memorable times become a record of particular occasions that otherwise could be lost. Writing your thoughts and feelings about your grandson's birth or your granddaughter's elementary school graduation become invaluable records of significant occasions. We also need to document some day-to-day events. Keep a notebook or start a file of daily memories. Jot down a few words about putting your grandchildren to bed or enjoying a family dinner so these experiences can be remembered for years to come. Also, it is a good idea to write your testimony, which we will discuss in the next chapter. All these accounts become part of our family legacy.

Blessing your children and grandchildren is the third reason for leaving a written legacy. Written blessings record words of affirmation, hope, and promise that may outlive us. When we have passed on to heaven, written blessings can live on to speak God's vision to our loved ones. Too often this means of affirmation on behalf of the Lord is missing in our culture. Writing a blessing is a powerful legacy to pass to the next generation. We will examine "The Blessing" at the end of this chapter.

Love Messages Lay the Foundation

A few years ago, I read *Letters from Dad*, written by Greg Vaughn. In the book, he conveys the importance of writing letters to our loved ones. After his dad's death, Vaughn realized the only possession he had from his dad was an old, rusty tackle box. Filled with anger, Vaughn stared at the tackle box. The Lord spoke to him: "If you were to go home to be with the Lord today, what would your loved ones hold in their hands tomorrow that would let them know they were the treasures of your life?"[20] Vaughn recognized that his family would have nothing tangible to remember his love for them. Thus began an incredible journey.

Vaughn contacted a dozen friends. He asked them if they had a letter of love and blessing from their dad. Not one of them replied yes. Next, he asked them how they would feel about such a letter if they had one. "Priceless" was the response. Vaughn then posed a third question: "Have you written such a love letter to your family?" Sadly, this time the answer was a unanimous no. These twelve men gathered to do what most men hate to do—write letters to their loved ones. The process began with letters to their wives, then to their children, and finally to their parents. What began as one letter developed into a monthly program of teaching men to write letters of love and blessing.

Today, churches throughout our country use this program to help men write to their families. *Letters to Dad* is an excellent resource that can encourage and equip adults to share intimate thoughts and feelings with the special people God has placed in their lives.

The Greatest Love Letter

Of course, our heavenly Father wrote the best love letter of all time to each of us. In His immeasurable love and wisdom, He wrote the Bible. What an astonishing example of sharing your heart in printed form so people for many generations could read it. I am always amazed that the Lord knew hundreds of years ago that I, Cathy Jacobs, would need certain knowledge in the twenty-first century. By writing His wisdom, He made sure I would know it. He did not rely on oral tradition. He appointed certain people to write His message so I could know His truths. What a striking role model He is for every parent and grandparent.

What You Can Do

Like Greg Vaughn, we can write meaningful messages to our children and grandchildren. We can leave something of lasting value to our loved ones by letting them know they are treasured. In doing so, we become a vessel through which the Lord overflows to our families. Perhaps they will be kept for future generations to see.

Vaughn said, "I've learned I can make a difference in the lives of my family. So can you. The marching orders do not come from me. The orders come from God Himself, written in His love letter to us called the Bible."[21] Vaughn goes on to say, "My passion will be to leave a godly legacy of faith, hope, and love to those precious ones I call my family."[22]

Written legacies take shape in various forms. You can be simple, direct, or creative. The mission is to write special messages conveying love from the Lord and from you. I believe there are four types of written legacies:

- letters, notes, messages
- prayers
- journals or scrapbooks
- blessings

Letters, Notes, Messages

The first and most obvious way to leave a written legacy is through letters, notes, or messages. The goal is to put in printed form words that convey your unconditional love and living faith. At times, you may want to give your children or grandchildren hope in a challenging season. Or you may want to scribble a quick note commending a certain trait or characteristic.

Recently, I sent a thank-you note to my grandson Caleb, commending him on one of his outstanding traits. I have my house on the market to sell. While Caleb was visiting me one day, a prospective buyer made an appointment to see the house. Without any hesitation, my six-year-old grandson helped me prepare the house for the showing. Later, I wrote him this note:

Dear Caleb,

Yesterday you were so helpful to me. With energy and strength, you helped me clean up my house. I am very thankful that Jesus made you big and strong. He also gave you a kind heart full of love for Him. Thank you for helping me.

I love you,
Nina

As you can see, the letters do not need to be long or complicated. In fact, brevity is recommended. One page is optimal; you can easily write more letters at another time. Start with simple words of encouragement. It may be most effective if the messages are handwritten. But if you are not comfortable writing by hand, then typing the words followed by your handwritten signature is a close second.

These written messages can be scribed any time, any day. Holidays are an excellent time to write a message—if you have time. I like to write a personal note on birthdays. Last year on my middle son's birthday, I wrote this message:

My dearest Gregory,

Happy birthday to a special son! Know that from the day you were born to the sweet days you were a little boy running from the bus stop into my arms to these days of eating lunch together as adults, I have treasured every moment with you. I love you.

Know that as long as there is breath in your lungs and a beating heart in your chest, God has a purpose for your life and a plan for you on this ear.th. He longs for you to know Him. May you be able to do so by reading His special words written just for us today.

Happy birthday! May you be blessed with many more.

Love always,
Mom

Valentine's Day is another appropriate time to send a written message of your unconditional love. Anniversaries, graduations, or vacations can also be moments to share a few intimate words. Maybe the needs of one of your children or grandchildren lay heavy on your heart. Send them a letter or note. Remember this is a journey to leave a legacy that outlives you.

When my loved ones are struggling with life, sometimes I may write or text a short note:

Dear Son,

Know that I am praying for you today as you go to work. My prayer is that the Lord will be your Way Maker, clearing the way of any obstacles in your path. Know that His face is shining down on you as you as go through this day. Remember how much I love you.

Mom

Whether you are a mom or a dad, a grandmom or a grand-dad, *Letters from Dad* is an exceptional guide for writing letters. Vaughn devotes an entire chapter to "The Lost Art of Letter Writing." He begins the chapter by saying, "There's no such thing as a bad letter that ends with the words 'I love you.'"[23] Usually, the biggest challenge is getting started. Put some words on paper (or computer). Nothing is cast in stone. Anything can be rewritten. This letter is not for an English grade. It is a means to express meaningful words.

Vaughn also includes two appendices to aid his readers in their letter writing. Appendix A in his book gives examples of various types of letters. Appendix B in his book is a collection of insights from Dr. Reg Grant of Dallas Theological Seminary, an experienced letter writer.

In *When They Turn Away*, Rob Rienow gives some outstanding guidelines for writing letters. He lists powerful words and phrases that are helpful in constructing a memorable letter. Some of Rienow's suggestions are listed below:[24]

- I love you no matter what.
- I am proud of you just because you are you.
- I'll always love you no matter what you do.
- I believe in you.
- I'm praying for you.
- I'm committed to you for the rest of my life.
- I'll never turn my back on you.

A few years ago, I wrote a short letter to my son-in-law who was searching for the next step in his life:

Dear Nate,

How proud I am of you! These past few months have been a series of ups and downs. I'm sure there have been some discouraging moments. But you have stayed close to the Lord seeking His best. Know that I love you no matter where the Lord leads you. I firmly believe the Lord will reveal His best to you when His time is right. Meanwhile, I am here for you and praying for you every day.

Love always,
Nina

Prayers

A second way to leave a written legacy of love is through prayers. Just as in writing notes or messages, prayers can be written for holidays, special days, or even those "no-big-deal" days. They can be short and simple. Say whatever is on your heart. Sometimes I write a special prayer for Christmas Day. Or

I may write a prayer to my loved ones on Valentine's Day, their birthday, or New Year's Day. One year I wrote the following prayer to all my children that I read at our family dinner:

Dear Jesus,

As we begin the New Year, I pray for my children and grandchildren. Please give them joy and peace as they start this season. Open their eyes to ways to love and serve You whether they are at work or at school. Help them to know they are Your hands and feet. Most of all, Lord, give each of them a heart to know You as their Lord and Savior. Bless them, Lord, with Your favor. In Jesus' name, I pray. Amen.

Often I write a prayer for the first day of school or a new job. I may write a short prayer on the last day of school or a job. These prayers can be texted or emailed. But I think the most special way is to "snail mail" the prayers. Everyone, even grown children, likes to receive a letter in the mailbox. Recently, I wrote the following prayer for a dear friend to share with her granddaughter who was leaving for college:

Dear Jesus,

Please be with my granddaughter as she leaves for college for the first time. May she always remember four things: 1) I love her with all my heart; 2) My love for her is a picture of God's huge love for her. He gave me to her so that she could see and feel what big love is; 3) God chose her before this world was created. He created her with a big smile on His face; 4) He has a plan to prosper her, not to harm her in any way. He always has her back no matter where she goes. In the precious name of Jesus, I pray, amen.

There are two other avenues for writing prayers. The first one is to use a handwritten prayer journal. Usually, I keep these prayers in chronological order. But you may organize a notebook with individual sections for each loved one. Another avenue is to type your prayers on the computer. Like the prayer journal, you may have one file where all prayers are kept in chronological order. Or you may establish separate files for each loved one.

Sometimes my prayers are eloquently written. Other times, I jot down concerns or sudden thoughts. At times, I do not even use complete sentences. I can embellish the written prayer later if I feel it is necessary. I always record the date I write the prayer. Sometimes I explain the circumstances that prompted the prayer. As time passes, I may write an addendum to some prayers as my loved one's needs increase or change. When God answers these prayers, I record in red ink how and when He worked.

One of my goals is to print out the prayers I have written and give them to my loved one. Sometimes I email or text the prayer after I have prayed it. Other times I wait for a special occasion, such as Christmas or Valentine's Day. I roll the prayer(s) into a scroll and wrap it with a bow. I then give the prayer scroll to my child or grandchild to show that I prayed for him or her. Prayer scrolls become a written record of the Lord's provision, as well as a written legacy of my love.

Journals and Scrapbooks

How much do you know about your parents and grandparents? Would you like to know more? I would. I wonder what life was like for my mom on the farm or for my dad in his family's grocery store. Maybe there are family stories that have never been told to your loved ones. Composing journals or creating scrapbooks is a third way to leave a written legacy of love to your children and grandchildren. You are sharing a heritage that belongs to all of your descendants. These family stories deserve to be passed to future generations.

Journals can be composed in various ways. You can write every day or you can write sporadically. A dear friend, Diane Harper, told me that she writes in a journal throughout the year. Each December, she collects her journaling and assembles it in a scrapbook. Diane adds pictures to illustrate her family stories. On Christmas Day, she gives each of her grown daughters a scrapbook with blank pages at the end. Her girls know that the following year additional stories and pictures will be added to those blank pages. The scrapbooks have become treasured gifts Diane's daughters look forward to receiving each year.

It is easy to become overwhelmed by journaling. You may think you do not have the ability or time to undertake such a project. But journaling does not need to be intimidating. You can tailor the journaling to your style, available time, and ability. Keep it simple. If you determine a schedule that fits your life-style, this treasured project becomes possible. Do what you can when you can. Anything is better than nothing.

Several Christmases ago, I made a scrapbook for each of my grown children. I kept the project simple. My goal was to share some pictures and a few comments about my life as a little girl. At the end of the scrapbook, I listed some topics I planned to explore with them in the future. Each scrapbook had eight pages. I wrote only about my life as a little girl, including a paragraph about each of my parents, my sister, and my pets. I described my home, especially my room, as well as short stories about family vacations and Christmas holidays.

The important point is to start writing! You don't have to write about every occasion or event. Hit the highlights. Tell about milestones or major events in your life. Pick a topic: holidays, vacations, and birthdays. Write about things that make you laugh or things that make you sad; write about the present, as well as about the past. I look forward to continuing that scrapbook at a later date, and I plan to add a section that covers my hopes and dreams for each of my children and grandchildren.

These written histories are invaluable family treasures. I cherished reading my grandmother's letters to my mom. I gleaned insights not only about my grandmother but also about my mother's college days. Mama and I had special conversations about those letters. Now that she is deceased, I treasure both the letters and the conversations.

There are also numerous electronic versions of journaling or scrapbooking. I prefer the hard copies that I assemble, but I have seen the beautiful electronic versions other grandparents have created.

These books can give roots to your children and grandchildren. One day there may be a grandchild, niece, or someone unknown to you who will be blessed by your family stories.

The Blessing

The fourth way to leave a written legacy of love is The Blessing. The Blessing is an ancient biblical practice. It is asking for God's favor on a person. The first action God takes after creating Adam and Eve is to bless them. In this initial blessing, I believe God communicates three elements to Adam and Eve. First, He speaks well of them. Next, He explains He has created them for a purpose; therefore, they are important. Third, by giving Adam and Eve a purpose, God gives them fulfillment and joy in life.[25]

The most profound blessing is the spoken blessing. It is so important that Matthew, Mark, *and* Luke recorded the moment when God the Father spoke a blessing over His beloved Son, Jesus, as Jesus was being baptized (Matthew 3:17, Mark 1:11, Luke 3:22). Writing a blessing to loved ones is also powerful. Some people write their blessings before speaking them. The Spoken Blessing is compelling. Therefore, it is worthy to write it down for my loved ones to keep. Sometimes I frame it or put it in a special book.

For example, recently I took my grandson on an overnight trip to celebrate his thirteenth birthday. We had a great time together. Before we returned home, I spoke the following words of a special blessing, based on Ephesians 2:10, I had written for him:

> Dear Nathaniel, as we celebrate your thirteenth birthday, know that you are God's masterpiece! You are an amazing young man because you were created anew in Christ Jesus. He has already planned good works for you to do in the future. I look forward to walking by your side in the years to come as you discover God's distinctive plans for you.

I gave Nathaniel a written copy of this special spoken blessing in a Memory Book I compiled for him after the overnight.

Words are powerful. They have the potential to bless or curse, to give life or death. Cavin Harper writes, "To bless literally means to 'speak well of another.'"[26] In his workshop, "Unleashing the Power of the Spoken Blessing," Harper says *blessing* means "to praise your loved one, to endow with God's favor and protection."[27] A blessing communicates to your children and grandchildren how treasured and valued they are, not only in your eyes but also in the Lord's eyes.

The blessing is not to be confused with praying. When we pray, we are speaking to the Lord on behalf of our loved ones: "Dear Jesus, please help my granddaughter to be a good friend to her classmates at school today." When we bless, we are speaking to our children and grandchildren on behalf of God. God is the source of the blessing. We are His conduits communicating His truths for their lives: "Dear Ella, you are a special young lady created by God to be sensitive and loving to your friends." I often write a blessing only after I prayed and asked the Lord to show me His thoughts for my grandchild.

The purpose of the blessing is to boost a person's self-worth, not his self-esteem. You promote a person's self-esteem when you compliment them on his or her abilities, appearance, or accomplishments: "Carrie, you are a good mother. You are caring and sensitive as you lead your family through life every day." You build a person's self-worth when you connect her strengths to God's creation of her: "Carrie, God has given you a tender heart that perseveres in loving and caring for your family every day." A person is beautiful, athletic, or smart because God has given him these attributes. When you speak a blessing over a loved one, you want to link their abilities to God's purpose for him.

When we give a blessing over a loved one, we affirm his God-given purpose, gifts, and personality. Our children and grandchildren are who they are because God made them that way. When we speak or write words of blessing in genuine love and sincerity, the blessing becomes compelling.[28] Such words enable our children and grandchildren to understand who they are because of God's purpose for them. These words are worthy of being spoken or written repeatedly throughout their lives.

Recently, my son, Jeff, and his wife, Kristin, moved from South Carolina to Pennsylvania to go to seminary. After loading the moving van with all their possessions, they were ready to leave. I spoke the following words, based on Proverbs 3:5-6, that I had written for them the previous night:

Dear Jeff and Kristin,

Since you are God's beloved children, know that the Lord has called you to this new chapter in life. Remember He has prepared you for this special time. May you trust in Him with all of your heart. Do not lean on your own understanding. But in all your ways seek Jesus. Then He will bless you as He makes your paths straight. Remember I am always here for you. I love you.

Several years ago, John Trent and Gary Smalley wrote *The Blessing*. In this book, Trent and Smalley explain that there are five elements to a blessing. In *Courageous Grandparenting*,

Cavin Harper presents the blessing in a simpler form, effectively condensing the five elements into three.[29] The first element is to communicate the high value of your child or grandchild. Tell your loved one he is special because he was created by God. The second element is to picture for them a special future. God created each person with a particular purpose. He has a plan for every person's life. The third element is to declare your unconditional commitment to supporting and directing your child or grandchild into God's purpose. When spoken, these elements are often accompanied by an appropriate, meaningful touch. You might place your hand on your loved one's head or shoulder. Or you might hold his hand while speaking your blessing.

There are two categories of blessings. There are blessings given on general occasions, such as bedtime or before a loved one leaves your home. Sometimes when I am putting my grandchildren to bed, I will lay my hand on their heads or shoulders and speak a few simple words: "May the Lord bless you tonight as you go to sleep. May the Lord of peace give you peace as you sleep. May He give you rest such that you wake up tomorrow morning refreshed and ready for a new day. Remember that 'Nina' is here for you every day and every night." These blessings can be repeated as the situation reoccurs.

Also, there are blessings given on special occasions, such as a birthday, an anniversary, or a graduation. These blessings are more specific and may be more personal. When my granddaughter graduated from elementary school last spring, I wrote her a blessing:

Dear Ella,

As you leave elementary school, remember four things: (1) Remember the talents that God has given you. He gave them to you for a reason. Use them. (2) Remember to be a good force for God. This is your mission here on earth. (3) Remember the only thing that matters is "Thy will be done!" Seek God's best and God's glory. (4) Always remember how much I love you. I am here for you every day. Call me. Come stay with me. Bring a friend. Or come alone. Both are treasures for me.

Love,
Nina

Other special occasions for specific blessings are the birth, baptism, or salvation of your child. You can also write a special blessing for the beginning of the school year, new career, first house, marriage, or other milestone.

When my oldest son got married last winter, I wrote a special message to this cherished groom and his bride that I shared on the eve of their wedding. The last paragraph of my words to Chris and Lauren were a short blessing: "And so, I lift my glass and my heart to my two sweet children. I've loved you from the start. May God bless you and keep you, and pour out all of His grace as you seek to serve Him, looking full into His face."

As the mother and grandmother, my desire is to write blessings to my grown children and grandchildren throughout all their lives. Cavin Harper states that since the father is the spiritual head of the household, the blessings he writes and speaks are of the most importance. Certainly, the ideal is for both grand-parents to write and speak blessings to their loved ones.

One of the most well-known blessings is recorded in Numbers 6:24–26. It is referred to as The Aaronic Blessing since it is a blessing given by the Lord to Aaron to speak over the Israelites. I know many grandparents who write or speak these words to their loved ones:

"[May] the Lord bless you and keep you;
[May] the Lord make his face shine upon you and be gracious to you;
[May] the Lord turn his face toward you and give you peace."

In his workshop, Harper explains the profound meaning of this beloved blessing. He says that as you write the first line, you are seeking God's protection over your loved one. When you write the second line, you are asking for God's pleasure to fall upon this person. As you write the final line, you are seeking God's full attention, His *shalom*, to be poured over your grand-child or grown child.[30]

You may also refer to other parts of the Bible. Scattered throughout the Old and New Testaments are many beautiful blessings. In fact, most of Paul's letters in the New Testament either start or end with a blessing. My favorite one is found in Romans 15:13, which says, "May the God of hope fill you with all joy and peace as you trust in him, so that you may overflow with hope by the power of the Holy Spirit." (See Appendix D for more blessings from the Bible.)

As a grandparent or parent, you are in a unique position

to nurture and strengthen your grandchildren and grown children through your words of blessing. Do not be intimidated by The Blessing. As you speak or write these powerful words, you become God's vessel through which He communicates to your loved ones words of love, acceptance, and protection. The blessing is His vision for their lives based on their unique qualities, talents, and attributes. Living in a turbulent world that often tears down God's vision, it is vital to speak God's blessings over your loved ones. Record these blessings so that God's purpose and plan for your children and grandchildren may be remembered throughout all their days.

A Fading Practice

One day you will be in heaven with the Lord. What will your children and grandchildren on earth hold in their hands to remember your love and God's blessing for them? If you desire to be an agent of powerful change in the lives of your loved ones, write your messages of love, record your family stories, and inscribe blessings from the Lord. This sixth key is part of a strong foundation for intimate relationships that pave the way for the highest calling on your life as a grandparent, pointing your children and grandchildren toward their heavenly Father.

Key Six: Leave a Written Legacy of Love

"Let this be written for a future generation, that a people not yet created may praise the Lord."

PSALM 102:18

119

"Thank You, heavenly Father, for this precious child that You and I love so much. Bless and keep him/her as the apple of Your eye, in the palm of Your hand and under the protection of the shadow of Your wing. In Jesus' name, I pray. Amen."

Rosanne Brasington,
Grandmother and friend

Study Questions

Chapter Seven: Pencils, Notebooks, and Computers

Pounding It Out

1. What are the three reasons to write messages to your loved ones? [1) To affirm and to encourage them, 2) to preserve family stories, 3) to bless them]

2. What are the three most important words in any language? ["I love you"] Did your parents write these words to you? Did your grandparents? How often do you write "I love you" to your children and grandchildren? Do you think you should write these words more often? How can you do that? When?

3. What are four ways to leave a well-written legacy to your children and grandchildren? [1) Write letters, notes, messages; 2) write prayers; 3) write a faith journal or make a scrapbook; 4) write a blessing] Which of these four ways is the easiest way for you to leave a written legacy? When can you start leaving a well-written legacy of love?

4. Letters, messages, or notes are good ways to express unconditional love. When was the last time you told your children or grandchildren that you are proud of them apart from anything they have done? How frequently do you tell them you love them just because of who they are?

5. Take a few minutes to write a note or letter to a loved one. Be sure to include in the note that you love this

person just because of who he or she is. Refer to Bob Rienow's guidelines for writing letters given in this chapter.

Driving It Home

1. Are you passing a legacy of brokenness, hurt, or pain to your loved ones by not saying "I love you"? If so, do you want to break this cycle within your family? Take a few minutes to pray to the Lord and seek His healing so your loved ones can know you love and cherish them. This is a legacy of wholeness and healthiness. Use the following prayer as a guide:

   Dear Father in heaven, I ask for Your inner healing so I may move beyond negative family history and patterns in my life. Give me Your grace and power to start a new legacy of sharing a love message to my family—a message they need and deserve to hear. Amen.

2. Read the following blessings. Pick one to write to a loved one or write your own.

   The Priestly Blessing

   "May the Lord bless you and keep you, May the Lord make his face shine upon you and be gracious to you, May the Lord turn his face toward you and give you peace."

   NUMBERS 6:23–26

Rosanne's Blessing

"Thank You, heavenly Father, for this precious child that You and I love so much. Bless and keep him/her as the apple of Your eye, in the palm of Your hand and under the protection of the shadow of Your wing. In Jesus' name I pray, amen."

A Blessing (sung to the tune of "Edelweiss")

"May the Lord, mighty God, bless and keep you for- ever. Grant you peace, perfect peace, joy in every endeavor. Lift your eyes and see God's face. Know His grace forever. May the Lord, mighty God, bless and keep you forever."

TELL YOUR STORIES

Key Seven: Pass Your Faith

"I love to tell the story; 'Twill be my theme in glory
To tell the old, old story of Jesus and His love."[31]

The church I attended as a child had a center aisle. On either side of it were rows of beautiful, dark mahogany pews. At the end of the aisle was a white marble altar. On it stood a majestic platinum cross. Framing the altar were large stained-glass windows. On sunny days, red and blue sunbeams danced on the floor.

My family was Lutheran, and we lived into our denomination's reputation of the "singing church." Today, sweet memories of singing the grand hymn, "I Love to Tell the Story," resonate within me. It was one of my favorite songs. My mother sang it with all her heart, and my tender, young spirit was touched.

What a blessing to sing this hymn with my mother. She was a faithful follower of Jesus Christ. But as a member of what is sometimes called the "Silent Generation," she did not speak easily about her faith. Still, I believe she loved to tell the story in the best way she knew.

Many grandparents struggle in a similar way. We long to tell our loved ones about the Lord. But we do not know how. A grandparent has numerous jobs and opportunities, but the greatest task is sharing the Good News of Jesus Christ with our loved ones.

A Most Challenging Conversation

The seventh and final key to passing a legacy of faith in Jesus Christ to your children and grandchildren is to tell your faith stories. We have studied six keys to equip our hearts and minds for the most important conversation of all—telling His story to our loved ones. The previous chapters helped to prepare us for this God-designed task of pointing the hearts of our loved ones toward their Savior, Jesus Christ.

For many grandparents, this conversation is challenging. Perhaps we grew up in church communities that did not model telling the gospel. That was the job of the pastors or Sunday school teachers. When my children were young, I assumed my parental task was to *get* my children to church. I expected church leadership to bring them into God's kingdom. Over the past few decades, many young people have abandoned their faith. But, as discussed in Chapter One, the most influential person over the heart of a child is the parent. Grandparents are second.

Embracing the Faith

As my children grew older, I sought the Lord for the best way to share the gospel with them. I had embraced faith in Jesus Christ as my savior when I was growing up. But as a parent, I struggled to help Carrie, Chris, Greg, and Jeff connect with Christ. For years, I prayed diligently for their Sunday school teachers to open my children's hearts to God. As my four children reached adolescence, I prayed fervently for the youth pastor. I hoped he would be able to reach their hearts. In countless prayer times, I begged the Lord to raise up someone to direct their eyes toward Him. I prayed for everyone, anyone, who would speak words of faith into my children's lives. A few years ago, however, I learned it is *my* responsibility to speak these words to my children and to my grandchildren.

Of course, others can speak God's truth to them, too. I hope they do. But I have a God-given calling to share the love of Christ with the next generation of my family. It is a sacred privilege for me to tell them His story. Oh, how He longs to reach these precious children and grandchildren. He has chosen *me* to point their hearts toward Him. It is part of His divine plan of discipleship. As their mother and grandmother, I have a powerful influence over their sweet hearts.

Tell God's Story

If only one generation fails to tell God's story of redemption to their children and grandchildren, the message of God's love can be diminished or lost. We see this horrible debacle in the Old Testament. The leaders of Joshua and Caleb's generation neglected to tell the younger generation of the mighty ways God rescued and provided for them. The result is recorded in Judges Chapter Two: the next generation fell into disobedience and distanced themselves from the Lord.

Can you imagine Caleb's grandson not knowing that his grandfather scouted the Promised Land for Moses or the next generation of Israelites not knowing about the walls of Jericho falling down? It is almost impossible to fathom. The failure of these parents and grandparents reveals the urgency of sharing our God stories with our children and grandchildren. God tells us throughout the Scriptures to *remember* what He has done for us and then tell it to our families. In the fourth chapter of Joshua, we read about Joshua commanding the Israelites to stack twelve stones on the west bank of the River Jordan at Gilgal. The purpose of these stones was to remind future generations of the goodness of God and what He had done for them. Joshua says, "In the future, when your children ask you, 'What do these stones mean?' tell them … these stones are to be a memorial to the people of Israel forever" (Joshua 4:6–7).

Visualize the Hebrew grandchildren sitting around the dinner table with Grandpa. He says, "Jotham, it was amazing! You should have been there as we came to the River Jordan. We had traveled many miles and waited many years to enter the land promised to us by the Lord. But first we had to cross that rushing body of water. It was at flood stage. Yet as the priests carrying the ark of the covenant of the Lord stepped into the river, the water upstream stopped. Eventually, these priests stood in the middle of the river on dry ground. All of Israel passed by until the whole nation had completed the crossing on dry ground. Then Joshua, following the Lord's directions, appointed twelve men to each select a stone to be placed at Gilgal as a remembrance of the amazing things God had done for them" (Joshua 3:5–17).

Yes, it is vital to tell the powerful stories of God. I have told my family some stories of God's working in my life. One of the most memorable encounters with the Lord happened early in my marriage. A few weeks after the wedding, I came home one day from teaching school. When I checked the mail, I found a bank statement from my previous bank. I discovered on the statement that a deposit had been made for $250 to my account on the Monday morning following my wedding. Since I was on my honeymoon, I wondered how the deposit was made. I asked my dad if he had kindly put that money into my account. He had not. He called the bank to investigate the situation. The bank confirmed a deposit was made, but we were unable to determine who put the money into our account. Several days later, my husband's Volkswagen broke down when he was coming home from work. After being towed to a nearby auto shop, he was told the cost to repair the car was … yep, $250! This provision, I know, was a gift from the Lord." What a joy it is to share this story with my family in hope of strengthening their faith in Christ.

God's Instructions: Talk to Them

The Bible gives clear instructions on how to tell our God stories. In Deuteronomy 6:7, Moses says, *"Talk* to them!" (emphasis added). He describes four quality times for us to talk:

1. As "you sit at home," talk to your family. Your weekly schedule probably does not include sitting around the

house. But an excellent time to share your stories is during a meal. Perhaps this conversation might occur when children or grandchildren are visiting overnight or during a vacation. Maybe you could share your story on a holiday with family seated around the dinner table.

2. As you "walk along the road" could be translated as traveling in the car. Car time is a great opportunity to share a God story or talk to your children about the Lord's presence in your life. Ask them to turn off headphones and listen. They are a captive audience in the car.

3. "When you lie down" is bedtime. Often bedtime is challenging and hectic. I think the Enemy intentionally instigates chaos at this time of the day because children's hearts are open. It is worth persevering, even sacrificing your own comfort, to share a short God story as you are saying "good night."

4. "When you get up" can be a chaotic time, too. But even a word or two when children are getting dressed or eating breakfast can have eternal implications at this time of the day, when hearts and minds are fresh.

Moses gave these wise instructions to the Hebrew people as they prepared to enter the land that had been promised to their forefathers for hundreds of years. It was a pivotal moment. Since he would not be accompanying the Israelites into the Promised Land, Moses spoke these important words as his final instructions. He pleaded with these people so near and dear to his heart: "Hear, Israel, and be careful to obey so that it may go well with you and that you may increase greatly … as the Lord, the God of your ancestors, promised you" (Deuteronomy 6:3). Can you detect the urgency in his voice? He commands parents *and* grandparents to teach their children and their children's children, saying, "Do not forget the things your eyes have seen" (Deuteronomy 4:9).

These instructions are as important today as they were in the days of the Old Testament. If we as parents and grandparents desire for life to "go well" for our loved ones, then we should take these ancient words to heart and share our stories so that the powerful ways of God will not be forgotten. If we share them, the Bible promises, "Then they [will] put their trust in God" (Psalm 78:7).

Tell Your Story

To point the hearts of your children and grandchildren toward the Lord, start by telling them your story. Actually, your story *is* His story. How did you come to know the Lord? Were you young or were you an adult? Did something happen in church one Sunday, or were you in another place?

Regardless of when, where, or how you gave your heart to Christ, you have a story. A dear friend of mine, Sherry Schumann, who is a grandmother, author, and speaker, says, "Every Christian has a story inside them to tell. It is edited and published by God. Only you can tell your story."[32] First John 5:10 says, "Anyone who believes in the Son of God has this testimony in his heart."

In *Preparing My Heart for Grandparenting*, Lydia Harris writes, "God wrote your life story. It has meaning not only for you but also for the loved ones who follow you. There is a divine purpose for each chapter. Every scene has significance. As we tell our stories of God's presence in our lives to our children and grandchildren, we pass a rich spiritual legacy. We build the faith of our family. Meanwhile, we build our own faith as we remember what God has done in and through us."[33]

So start talking! How has God walked with you?

Sometimes as I kneel in prayer time with my grandchildren beside their beds, I share briefly the story about the morning I prayed in my home church for the Lord Jesus to come into my heart. It was a quiet moment. There were no flashing lights. Kneeling in the front pew, I prayed a short prayer at the beginning of the church service. After months of conversations with close Christian friends and the help of numerous Bible studies, I put aside my doubts and opened my life to God. As I tell about this significant time, I paint a picture for my little ones of the Lord God in heaven hearing my simple prayer.

Sometimes as I eat lunch with my grown son or as the kids and I ride in the car, I recount to them some of my "mountaintop" experiences. One of the most profound experiences I've had as a Christian came a few years ago at the Urbana Conference in St. Louis, Missouri. This gathering is a national conference for missionaries. I sat in the auditorium with thousands of Christians, most of whom were missionaries preparing to go into the mission field. The glorious moment came when we stood and sang the aged hymn, "Amazing Grace." I felt God's amazing love as I lifted my voice with the throngs of my brothers and sisters in Christ. The experience foreshadowed the glory of one day singing in heaven with all of God's people. I will never forget it.

As I share this special moment with my children and grandchildren, the Holy Spirit can give them a taste of magnificent times with Him.

I also become intentional about sharing the challenging times in my walk with the Lord. As hard situations arise in the lives of my family, I prayerfully seek opportunities to share with them the difficulties I have experienced. For example, as I watched my father battle Lou Gehrig's Disease (ALS), I clung desperately to my faith, seeking the Lord for guidance and comfort. As my father declined, I was unhappy with God's answers. I lay awake at night wondering if God could hear me. Slowly, the Lord revealed to me the glories of heaven. I did not want to let go of my dad, but, gradually, the Lord gave me the grace to release Daddy to Him.

Life is not always easy. God's answers are not always what we want to hear. But as I tell my family of this painful time when I debated with the Lord, the Holy Spirit can plant seeds of trust in their hearts.

Honesty is important when sharing God stories. We do not need to embellish or diminish any chapter of our lives that God has written. As we authentically share with our families our encounters with the Lord, the Holy Spirit builds a valid profession of faith that is worthy to be told to future generations.

Consider these three questions when you share your story:

1. What was your life like before you came to know Christ?
2. What happened to change your life?
3. How is your life different now?

For example, here is my story outline. I was raised in a Lutheran church. I went every Sunday with my parents. I was very involved. As a teenager, I was the president of my youth group. I learned much about The Almighty God. But this was formal and felt cold to me.

In college, a friend told me about a personal relationship with Jesus Christ. I had never heard about a close connection with the Lord. My friend explained that Jesus longs to be my personal Savior and Lord. This news became intimate and warm. As a result, I joined various Bible studies and prayer groups. I intentionally sought opportunities to learn about Jesus Christ. Eventually, I prayed and asked the Lord to forgive me for my sins and to come into my heart. I discovered new meaning in the Scriptures as I read my Bible. I felt the presence of Christ in my life.

Years later, my husband left my family. I never saw divorce as a part of my life. I, Cathy Jacobs, the leader of Family Ministry at my church, had *my* family fall apart. I do not know what I would have done if the Lord had not walked alongside me through such a terrible time. He still guides me every day.

Bare Bones

The three paragraphs above contain the bare-bones version of my God story. Many times you have only a few minutes to share your testimony with a loved one. Be prepared to tell your story in three to five minutes. You can always embellish it later.

Picture tucking your grandchild into bed one night. He may ask you, "Grandma, is God real?" Pow! God has given you a moment or two to share your story with this little one. You do not have time for a long explanation. He will be asleep soon. But in three to five minutes you can say, "Yes, God is real. I know because one day He came into my life." Then answer the three questions in a simple, short manner.

Maybe your entire family comes to your home for Thanksgiving dinner. During the meal, tell them you want to share an important experience with them. In a *few* minutes, share with them how Jesus became a part of your life. You will lose some listeners if your story is too long.

Maybe one day a loved one will ask you a question. You may have more time to share your story. Use your bare-bones version as an outline and add details, commenting about your feelings. This can become a powerful story that impacts your grown child or grandchild.

Hopefully, the Lord will use the short version of your testimony to open doors for additional conversations. At those times, you may expand your story, giving more details and sharing more feelings. Meanwhile, prepare the bare-bones story. Remember the three questions and answer gently. I suggest you write down your story. Share it several times with a friend or neighbor so that you will be prepared to tell the account of "the hope" that lives within you (1 Peter 3:15).

Subsequent Stories

Often your bare-bones salvation story is your first opportunity to share God's love with your children. Subsequent God stories could include a time when a desperate or fervent prayer was answered. Or discuss a time when the Lord met a significant need. Share your favorite Bible story with your grandchildren.

Why is it your favorite one? How has God revealed Himself to you in this story? When have you felt God's presence in your life? Has the Lord sustained or healed you of a serious illness? What did you learn about God during that experience?

Share honestly where and how God has been a part of your life. This testimony to the Lord's faithfulness demonstrates to your loved ones His presence on earth and in people's lives. Let them know that what God has done for you, He can do for them. Teach them God loves them, chose them to be His, and longs to be invited into their lives. One day they, too, can have God stories to share.

Leading Your Loved One into a Relationship with Jesus

Sharing your God stories may open the door for more spiritual conversations. Perhaps you will notice your child's heart is ready to receive the salvation Christ offers. If so, grab the opportunity and lead him into prayer. This is the most precious conversation you can have with your loved one. It is the highest calling on your life. Know that the Lord is with you as you speak. He is closer to you than your next breath. The power of opening your loved one's eyes to God does not depend on you; the power of the Holy Spirit leads a person to Jesus.

Many grandparents wonder how to lead their children or grandchildren to Christ. Frequently, we are intimidated by this divine opportunity. Even though it is profoundly important, it is not difficult. If you are feeling overwhelmed, know that the Enemy is feeding you a lie. Satan will attempt to tell us we are unable to share the Good News of Christ with our children.

Recognize his lie. Remember the powerful presence of the Holy Spirit within you. Pray and ask the Lord to be with you, guide you, and give you His words for this precious loved one. (See Appendix E: Tips for Sharing the Gospel with Children.)

If you have given your heart to the Lord, you can lead your children and grandchildren into a relationship with Jesus Christ by walking them through the following steps:

1. Explain God made him and loves him very much (John 3:16 and Romans 8:38–39).
2. Make clear that no matter how hard he may try to be a good person, he will make mistakes. No one is perfect. Sin is anything he says, does, or thinks that separates him from God. When he admits these sins, God wipes away all the sins (Romans 3:23, 5:12, and 6:23).
3. Tell him Jesus left heaven and lived a sinless life on earth so He could take the punishment we deserve (1 Peter 2:24 and Romans 5:8).
4. Teach him Jesus rose to give him new life! (John 5:24 and 2 Corinthians 5:17). He can trust Jesus and become God's child (John 1:12 and 14:6).
5. Ask him if he is ready to trust Jesus as his Savior. If he says yes, then lead him in the following prayer:

"Dear Jesus, I have made many mistakes. No matter how hard I try, I cannot be perfect. But I believe You died and rose so I can live forever in heaven. Come into my life, Jesus. Forgive my sins and save me. I now place my trust in You alone for my salvation. I accept Your gift of eternal life. Amen."

6. Finally, explain Jesus will live forever within him through the Holy Spirit (Galatians 2:20). The Holy Spirit will guide him in the ways he should go (John 16:13).

7. One day, at God's appointed time, he will go to live in God's heavenly home that has been prepared especially for him (Luke 23:43).

8. Get a piece of paper. Write on the paper "Today [loved one's name] gave his life to Jesus." Date the paper. Sign your name. Have your child or grandchild sign his name. When possible, give your child an age-appropriate Bible. You can tape this piece of paper inside the front cover as a forever reminder of this eternal moment. Encourage your loved one to keep this Bible as concrete evidence of Jesus coming into his heart. In the days and years ahead, when he may be struggling, he can look at the piece of paper and remember God's entry into his life.

In summary, your loved one needs to know these four truths:

1. God loves him and has a special plan for his life.
2. Your loved one, like everyone, has sinned.
3. Jesus Christ died to redeem his sins.
4. To receive the gift of salvation and learn of God's wonderful plan for his life, your loved one must confess his sins and put his faith in Jesus Christ.

At the moment of your loved one's salvation, the angels in heaven rejoice over the homecoming of a precious soul! (See Luke 15:10.) The moment is particularly special because you, the parent or grandparent, have ushered this child into God's holy kingdom. For all the love you may have for this person, know that God loves him more than you can imagine. Also, remember this has not been *your* project. Instead, know that the Lord has used you as His instrument to reach the heart of His dear child. You were His vehicle used by His Holy Spirit. Shout halleluiah! Then fall to your knees and thank Him for allowing you to be His instrument.*

Their Stories

Steven Green wrote a beautiful song, "Find Us Faithful." The chorus's lyrics encourage us to leave a legacy of faithfulness for those who follow us.[34] One day our earthly lives will be a memory. Let us make sure the memory is a glorious one that reflects the love of God. May our families remember not only a good grandparent but also a godly grandparent. Strive to be a life changer in the lives of your loved ones so that you are a grandparent who makes a significant difference. Tell your children and grandchildren all you have seen God do. Share His unchanging truths in your life. Pray with them to receive Christ into their hearts. Let your loved ones know that you love them and so does the King of the Universe, the Almighty God. He is waiting now for them to become a citizen of His kingdom so He may write their stories.

Key Seven: Pass Your Faith

"We will not hide them from their descendants; we will tell the next generation the praiseworthy deeds of the Lord, his power, and the wonders he has done." Psalm 78:4

"Even when I am old and gray, do not forsake me, my God, till I declare your power to the next generation, your mighty acts to all who are to come."

PSALM 71:18

"Then we your people, the sheep of your pasture, will praise you forever; from generation to generation we will recount your praise."

PSALM 79:13

*There are many excellent books available on leading your child to Christ. Three of my favorites are *I Believe in Jesus* by John MacArthur, *My John 3:16 Book: Lola Mazola's HappyLand Adventure* by Robert J. Morgan, and *God's Great News for Children* by Rick Osborne and Marnie Wooding. These colorful books are easy for children to understand. Another excellent resource for grandparents and parents is *Leading Your Kids to Christ: 30 Devotions to Prepare Parents* by Criswell Freeman.

Study Questions

Chapter Eight: Tell Your Stories

Pounding It Out

1. What is the most important conversation you can have with your children and grandchildren? [Telling your God stories] The previous six keys have been preparing you for this God-designed task of pointing your loved ones toward their savior, Jesus Christ. Is this a challenging conversation for you? Why or why not?

2. Who is the most influential person over the heart of a grandchild? [A parent] Who is the second most influential person? [A grandparent] Who called you, the grandparent, to share Christ's love with your children and grandchildren? [God—it is His divine plan of discipleship for parents and grandparents to point the hearts of their children and grandchildren toward Him]

3. If we tell our stories to our loved ones, what does God promise in Psalm 78:7? ["then they would put their trust in God and would not forget his deeds but would keep his commands"]

Driving It Home

1. Read Deuteronomy 6:7. When are the four times Moses tells us to talk to our children? [1) When you sit at home, 2) walk (or drive) along the road, 3) when you lie down aka bedtime, 4) when you get up in the mornings] When

is the easiest time of day for you to talk to your loved one? Which is the hardest?

2. What stories can you share with your loved ones about God's presence in your life? Be sure to answer the three questions Catherine lists as the bare-bones version of your stories:

> What was your life like before you came to know Christ?
> What happened to change your life?
> How is your life different now?

Write these stories. Pray for the Lord to provide a time for you to share your God stories with your loved ones.

3. Catherine states that if you have surrendered your heart to the Lord, you can lead your children and grandchildren into a relationship with Jesus. Review the nine steps of leading a loved one to Christ. Read the prayer in the sixth step to familiarize yourself with this short but life-changing prayer. During your daily babushka prayer time, ask the Holy Spirit to open opportunities for you to lead your family to Him.

CHAPTER NINE

MAKE A PLAN

"Intentionality in the context of grandparenting means to deliberately choose to live for the next generations as a conduit of God's grace and truth according to His purpose."[35]

Cavin Harper

If you desire to be a godly grandparent leaving a legacy of faith in Jesus Christ to your children and grandchildren, intentionality is essential. But first, let me tell you about my son Greg.

Like Grandfather, Like Grandson

Watching my children grow has been one of the most fascinating aspects of my life. I have seen four distinctly individual people emerge from my womb and take on the world. Each one has a unique personality along with a particular set of gifts and strengths. I see my mother-in-law's determination in my daughter, Carrie. My mom's sweet personality shines through my oldest son, Chris. My youngest son, Jeff, has a quick mind, which reminds me of his dad in medical school. But my third son, Greg, amazes me most of all. How can he be so much like my dad? He was only four years old when Daddy went home to be with the Lord.

My dad had a massive oak desk in his office, covered with multiple piles of papers. But each pile was neatly stacked. Not one piece of paper was out of place. In his bedroom closet, every article of clothing was carefully arranged. His dresser drawers, including his sock drawer, were immaculately ordered. I thought of my dad's meticulous tidiness recently as I walked into Greg's new home. Everything was in its place. Even his socks are intentionally organized.

Intentionality. Similar to my dad, Greg does everything methodically. Before starting a project, he develops a plan, keeping in mind the project's purpose. His thorough attention to detail takes time. So if you are in a hurry, he might not be your best man. But if success is your goal, he is the one to choose.

The Need for Intentionality

To be a life changer for your children and grandchildren, you need to be diligently intentional. Our world moves at a rapid pace. To be a grandparent who makes a difference, you must develop a plan and act accordingly. Otherwise, a week, a month, or even a decade will pass before you know it. In fact, a whole lifetime can slip by without accomplishing those all-important goals we long to achieve.

What is intentionality? In *Grandparenting with a Purpose*, Lillian Penner says it is being determined to speak, write, and behave in a certain way—to make sure things are done by design, on purpose.[36] Intentionality is becoming focused in order to bear the desired fruit. It is setting priorities. Many good choices are available to us as grandparents, so we must set specific grand-parenting goals to impact our loved ones in an eternal manner. Otherwise, the tyranny of the good will overpower our godly intentions, which means we will settle for what is good rather than strive for what is best.

How to Become Intentional

The first step in becoming an intentional grandparent is to con-centrate on the goals you desire to achieve. Setting priorities positions us to accomplish our goals. Priorities are the choices we set as precedents in our lives. They help us organize our goals and actions. Also, priorities help us to focus our efforts and time wisely. Then we act by design to produce the desired fruit.

When I study Scripture, I see that God seems to have three priorities. No matter who we are, where we are going, or how we are getting there, these three priorities can help us to live according to God's best plans.

The first priority is your relationship with God. Who do you truly serve? Is it the Lord, or is it money, power, or relationships? As discussed in Chapter Two, in seeking to be an intentional, godly grandparent, the first question you ask yourself is this: what is the status of my relationship with God? For example, are you spending quality time in worship, in prayer, and in His Word? Do you need to make some adjustments in your life so that you can love the Lord your God with all of your heart, mind, and soul?

The second priority is your relationship with your family.

This priority has three layers to it. First and foremost is your relationship with your spouse. Next to your relationship with the Lord, your relationship with your husband or wife is a top priority. God gave you this special person. In His wisdom, He knows the importance of giving this person your best, second only to the Lord. To be an effective life-changing grandparent, your second responsibility in life is to do all you can do to nurture your marriage. Too often, we Americans put the children and then grandchildren above our relationship with our husband or wife. Many adults also sacrifice their marriage on the altar of their job. When we succumb to either of these temptations, our marriage will suffer. Then our fruitfulness as a Christian is compromised. Eventually, this will impact our effectiveness as a grandparent.

After our relationship with our spouse comes our relationship with our children and then our grandchildren. It is easy to get these family priorities out of order. When we do, once again, we compromise the quality of our lives for the Lord, as well as our role as a godly grandparent.

The final layer of the second priority is your extended family. Seek the best relationship possible first with your parents, next with your siblings, and finally with your nieces, nephews, and cousins.

The third priority is your relationship with the world. What is your mission in life? God gifted you with certain strengths and abilities so you can live into your purpose in serving the world. Paul tells us we are God's "masterpiece," created by Him to do the good things He planned long ago for us (Ephesians 2:10, NLT). That is amazing! For many adults, their ministry is their occupation. Even though God planned our ministry years ago, we must be careful not to let our occupation dominate our thoughts or actions. It is often easy to let the demands of our career take precedence over our relationship with the Lord or with our families.

Take an Inventory

Knowing these priorities is helpful as we try to glorify God with our lives. From time to time, I look at the big picture of my life and ask some questions: Am I keeping my relationship with the Lord first? Am I keeping my relationship with my family in order? Am I keeping my ministry/job in its place, or am I allowing it to take over my other priorities? Do I need to make adjustments? I can focus so much on the day-to-day issues that I lose sight of the big picture. When I do, I may miss the mark God has for me. For example, I may be so involved in my ministry to grandparents that I miss my grandchild's music concert or a Saturday morning sporting event. I have to look at my calendar with an objective eye to see where my priorities are. Focusing on and keeping God's three priorities in place gives me a framework for my life so I am positioned to do what the Lord calls me to do.

Beware the Enemy

Our Enemy loves to interfere with these priorities. His number one priority (yes, even Satan has priorities) is to prevent us from living into the calling God has for each of us. John 10:10 says, "The thief comes only to steal and kill and destroy." Satan continually tries to confuse, misalign, or delete any (or all) of the priorities God ordained for us.

But Jesus comes "that [we] may have life, and have it to the full" (John 10:10). In John 10:14, Jesus tells us He is "the good shepherd." If we stay focused on the Lord through worship, reading our Bibles daily and praying fervently, we can stand strong against any influence the Enemy may cast our way. We can keep our priorities in order.

Recently, I was struggling to write a magazine article. Writing does not come easily for me. Tired and discouraged, I seriously thought of resigning from the assignment. But a good friend reminded me the Lord has called me to write at this time in my life. The next morning, I read my daily Bible devotion. It was based on Psalm 62:6— "He alone is my rock and my salvation; he is my fortress, *I will not be shaken*" (emphasis added). I said, "I will *not* quit." My next reading assigned for the day was from Philippians 3:12—"I press on to take hold of that for which Christ Jesus took hold of me." I prayed, "Okay, Lord, I will 'press on' to do what You have called me to do." Finally, I concluded my quiet time with the reading from *Praying God's Word: Day by Day* by Beth Moore: "Believe Him. Believe He can do what He says He can do. *And believe also that you can do what He says you can do*" (emphasis added).[37]

I was determined to complete the assignment. The Enemy was not going to discourage me. Writing at this time is my ministry. It is my third priority. I forged ahead and completed the article. Later, a pastor told me that one of his church members had been encouraged when she read my article. I smiled, realizing it was worth writing the article for the one grandmother who was inspired.

Establish Clear Goals

An intentional grandparent needs clear goals. We are to impact our families in light of God's standards, not our standards or the standards of society. A good coach would not go into a game without a plan. A godly grandparent should not live without an intentional plan. Take the time to pray, plan, and produce an intentional framework for living into your role as a grandparent. Achieving desired goals rarely happens by chance. It is almost always the result of good planning and diligent implementation.

What Is Your Plan?

How can you become intentional? What are you going to do tomorrow to align your loved ones with the divine destiny planned for them by God?

This is where The Seven Keys are helpful to me. Prayerfully, I go through each key open to the Holy Spirit to prick my heart at the point where I may need to act. Look at each key below and ask yourself the following questions:

1. Key One: Surrender Your Heart to the Lord. In order to pass a legacy of faith I must *be* a person of faith. Have I given my whole heart to the Lord? Am I putting Him first in my life? Is there an area today that I need to recommit to Him?

2. Key Two: Read the Bible Daily. Am I a "Rudy" each day? Do I run to be near my master? Do I read my Bible daily, seeking His words to me? Do I have a realistic plan for reading the Bible? Do I have a Bible that is easy

to read? Where is a quiet place for me to go consistently to spend time with the Lord in His Word?

3. Key Three: Pray Fervently. Have I taken on my babushka prayer mantle so that I pray diligently for each of my children and grandchildren? Do I need to set up a regular prayer schedule so that I spend quality and quantity time in prayer for each of my loved ones?

4. Key Four: Pursue Healthy Relationships. Do I spend quality time with each of my children and grandchildren? If they live a distance away, do I call or FaceTime with them on a regular basis? When was the last time I told each of them "I love you"?

5. Key Five: Heal Broken Relationships. Do I have a broken relationship with any of my children or grandchildren? Do I need to give or seek forgiveness from any one of them?

6. Key Six: Leave a Written Legacy of Love. Have I written a note, a prayer, or a blessing to my loved ones recently? Do any of my loved ones need to hear a special word of encouragement from me?

7. Key Seven: Pass Your Faith. Have I told my children and grandchildren the story of how I came to know the Lord? Have I told them Jesus loves them and has a special plan for their lives?

As I pray through The Seven Keys, I write down the areas I feel the Lord has brought to my attention. Sometimes I make a graph. Across the top of a page I write "Key One, Key Two, Key Three … Key Seven." Down the side of the page I write the names of my children and grandchildren. In the appropriate boxes, I briefly write the action step the Lord showed me in my prayer time for my loved ones. If needed, I make some notes at the bottom of the page. I put this sheet of paper in my quiet time notebook so I can reference it frequently.

This diagram helps me to see at a glance where I need to put my energies. It helps me develop a plan of what I feel God is calling me to do, so I can intentionally pass a legacy of faith to each of my children and grandchildren. It also helps me evaluate my priorities. Am I keeping my relationship with the Lord first? Am I keeping my relationships with my family members in order? Am I keeping my ministry/job in its place, or am I allowing it to take over my other priorities? By reviewing the diagram, I can see where I need to make adjustments.

Becoming an Intentional Life Changer

The culture in which our children and grandchildren are living is vastly different from the world in which we grew up. Yet somehow we grandmoms and granddads need to prayerfully and carefully step up. Cavin Harper says, "Intentionality presupposes that I am proactive about looking for ways to express [God's] purpose to bring blessing, not cursing, into my children's and grandchildren's lives."[38] Who else will fight for their hearts? Who can help them see beyond the next cell phone call or text? We must intentionally choose to be visionary for them. Being diligent grandparents enables us to set our priorities and become life changers, impacting generations to come. It is grandparents making a difference.

"Hear, O Israel: The Lord our God, the Lord is one. Love the Lord your God with all your heart and with all your soul and with all your strength. These commandments that I give you today are to be upon your hearts."

DEUTERONOMY 6:4-5

"Jesus replied: 'Love the Lord with all your heart and with all your soul and with all your mind.' This is the first and greatest commandment."

MATTHEW 22:37

Study Questions

Chapter Nine: Make a Plan

Pounding It Out

1. What is intentionality? [Being determined to speak, write, and behave in a certain way, understanding that things are done by design, on purpose] How important is intentionality in today's world? Why?

2. What "good" choices have you made that could interfere with your godly grandparenting goals? How can you be intentional to make sure you accomplish your grandparenting goals?

3. What are priorities? [Things we set as precedents in our lives that help us organize our goals and actions] What are the three main priorities in life? [1) Relationship with the Lord, 2) relationship with your family, 3) relationship with the world through your God-given ministry]. Take a few minutes to look at the bigger picture of life and ask yourself these questions:

   a. Am I keeping my relationship with the Lord first?
   b. Am I keeping my relationship with my family in order?
   c. Am I keeping my ministry or job in its proper place, or am I allowing it to take over my other two priorities?
   d. Do I need to make adjustments? If so, where? How? When?

4. What is Satan's number one priority? [To prevent us from living into the calling God has for each of us] Read John 10:10. Has Satan confused, misaligned, or deleted any of the priorities God ordained for you? Stop and pray now. Ask the Lord to defeat Satan and give you a full life.

Driving It Home

1. What is your plan to become intentional? Review the summary of The Seven Keys as listed in this chapter. Make a graph as described by Catherine. As you answer the questions listed with each key, fill in your graph. During your daily prayer time, ask the Holy Spirit to guide you in developing an intentional plan for impacting the lives of your children and grandchildren.

2. Catherine states that we are to impact our families in light of God's standards, not our standards. How is being an intentional grandparent similar to being a good coach? [Each has a game plan with clear goals]

CHAPTER TEN

Run, Grandparent, Run

A Candlelight Celebration

A dozen grandparents surrounded an elegant dining room table to celebrate the conclusion of their small group study on The Seven Keys. The room was hushed and the lights were low. In the center of the oval table, someone had arranged an eclectic collection of white candles. Some of the candles stood tall and majestic; others were small tea lights. After each grandparent lit one tall taper representing himself, he then lit one tea light to symbolize his spouse and each of his children and grandchildren. Also present was a single great-aunt with eight nieces and nephews. When the last person had lit his family's candles, twelve tapers shone softly. But the room was brilliant with light! Encircling the dozen towering candles were over *sixty* tea lights. Yes, the room was ablaze with candlelight.

I don't think anyone missed the significance of the moment. At least, I hope not. Only twelve humans stood in the room. But in the spiritual recesses of this expanse were sixty other people. Each one, precious and valuable, has been created by his or her heavenly Father. It is God's ultimate desire for each individual to live forever in heaven. As grandparents, we are to do everything within our ability to direct these loved ones God has entrusted to us toward their heavenly home.

The profoundness of the situation does not apply only to the future. There is a calling on each grandparent to impact every member of his family and bring each one into God's kingdom ASAP. The beauty and power of living with Christ begins, not in heaven but on earth. Each day a person walks with Jesus is a day full of divine potential. Without Christ reigning in their hearts, our descendants miss both their daily and eternal destiny.

God's Family Plan

We learn in the early verses of Genesis that God created the family (Genesis 1:27-28). As He molded and shaped each family, His ultimate vision was for each grown parent and grandparent to become a strong spiritual leader. God's plan is for each grandparent, as the matriarch or patriarch of a family, to guide his or her loved ones as they traverse this turbulent world. Remember Paul's words in 2 Timothy 4:7. We are to "fight the good fight," "finish the race," and "keep the faith" until the Lord takes us home to heaven. God never intended for us to retire in our senior years. Yes, there are seasons in life. We are probably not running the same race we ran in our forties or early fifties. But God has an unbelievable destiny for us in our later decades of life: to impact the hearts of our children and grandchildren, and bring them home to heaven. The goal is for us to spend eternity together.

God's Marching Orders for Grandparents

We grandparents may feel intimidated by God's calling. The first chapter of Joshua is composed of words that encourage us as we seek to live into our grandparenting roles. In verse nine, the Lord *commands* Joshua and His people to "be strong and coura-geous." He also says, "Do not be afraid; do not be discouraged." Why? Because, as it says in the last part of verse nine, "the Lord your God will be with you *wherever* you go" (emphasis added). We have nothing to fear because we have the mighty power of God with us everywhere we go.

In verse two, the Lord tells Joshua to "get ready." The time had finally come for the Hebrew people to enter the land prom-ised to their ancestors hundreds of years earlier. This is what you have been doing as you have read this book. You have been pre-paring to take the land the Lord gave you, that is, your families.

In verses three, five, seven, and eight, respectively, the Lord says:

- "I will give you every place where you set your foot."
- "No one will be able to stand against you all the days of your life. As I was with Moses, so I will be with you; I will never leave you nor forsake you."
- "Be careful to obey all the law my servant Moses gave you; do not turn from it to the right or to the left, that you may be successful wherever you go."

- "Meditate on it day and night, so that you may be
  careful to do everything written in it. *Then* you will be
  prosperous and successful" (emphasis added).

The Lord expects us to be strong and courageous. When we realize He is with us everywhere we go, we can intentionally impact the lives of our children and grandchildren. By God's grace and power, we are His instruments to reach the next generation. With our eyes fixed on Jesus, we are neither terrified nor discouraged. We move confidently as life changers to point our loved ones toward heaven.

But do not look to the left or to the right. It is easy to get distracted by the world, previous mind-sets, or earlier life habits. God calls us to remove these distractions and focus on His call to us as grandparents so we and our descendants can be "prosperous and successful."

A Word from the New Testament

The New Testament also has compelling advice and encouragement for grandparents: "Therefore, since we are surrounded by such a great cloud of witnesses, let us throw off everything that hinders and the sin that so easily entangles, and let us run with perseverance the race marked out for us" (Hebrews 12:1).

Those hindrances can be lies from the world. Or maybe old thoughts creep into your mind, causing you to think once again, *I can't do this! I'm not a pastor or Sunday school teacher. I'm only a grandparent.* The author of Hebrews tells us to "throw off" anything that may hinder us.

Also, we are told to eliminate the sin that so easily entangles us. What sin is keeping you from being all God called you to be? Be a Rudy and spend time with the Lord. Confess your wrongdoing to Him in your babushka prayer times, and ask Him to forgive you for anything that may be preventing you from following His plan for this season of your life.

I love the next line of this verse. It says to "run"! That is right. We are to "run with perseverance the race marked out for us ." It may not always be an easy race. But this race is not ordinary. The Lord has marked it out for us. With a great cloud of witnesses surrounding us, we can persevere.

Run with Perseverance

How do we persevere in this challenging, sometimes exhausting race? Look at the next verse in Hebrews: "fixing our eyes on Jesus, the pioneer and perfecter of faith. For the joy set before him he endured the cross, scorning its shame, and sat down at the right hand of the throne of God" (12:2).

When running the race of bringing all of our loved ones to heaven, we are to "fix" our eyes on Jesus. He is our focal point. He is fully capable of being the center of our attention because He is the pioneer and perfecter of our faith. For the joy set before Him, He endured the cross. Then He sat down at the right hand of the throne of God.

Jesus ran the race marked for Him. He knew the consequences of His obedience. He ran on our behalf, filled with joy at the reality of our redemption. After He had done all He was called to do, He was given the seat of highest honor, that of sitting at the right hand of the throne of God.

The race marked out for you is different from the race marked out for me. Each has its challenges and difficulties. But for the joy of the fruit of our labors, we need to throw off all that holds us back and run!

The third verse in Hebrews 12 gives us the motivation to persevere in this race: "Consider him who endured such opposition from sinners, so that you will not grow weary and lose heart" (v. 3).

Once again the author of Hebrews exhorts us to look to Jesus. He knew we could become weary, even lose heart. By staying in God's Word daily and falling to our knees as babushkas, we can keep our hearts and minds stayed on Christ. Then we will be strong and courageous. We can run this amazing race God marked out for us.

But Why?

Why do we become intentional grandparents? It takes considerable time and calculated effort to follow The Seven Keys. We have worked diligently all of our lives. Why not relax and simply enjoy this season of life?

The first reason is the Lord commands us to live intentionally in The Great Commission. In Matthew 28:19-20, Jesus calls us to make disciples of all the nations. Certainly, we are to be concerned for every people, every tribe, and every nation around the world. God's heartfelt desire is for all the people to be with Him forever. That is one reason God created families. His discipleship plan is for parents and grandparents to teach their children and grandchildren so that each and every one comes to Him. Our evangelistic duty begins at home. Our foremost mission field is our loved ones.

The second reason we seek to lead our loved ones into the kingdom is God's fulfillment of His purpose for our children and grandchildren. As the grandparents at the candlelight ceremony realized, each day without God reigning in the hearts of our loved ones is a day they are missing God's best plan, provision, and potential. Salvation does not begin in heaven. It starts the minute a person surrenders his heart to Christ. Jesus is the lover of their souls today, as well as forevermore. Starting today, we must fight for their hearts to be turned toward their Savior.

The third reason is the most important. As spiritual beings, we will live forever. Will we live in the glorious presence of the Lord, or will we live forever separated from Him? There is no third choice for us or for our loved ones.

Heaven is a real place. We are told in Revelation 21:3 that one day God will live with man. We will be His people and He will be our God. "Emmanuel" means "God with us." In this dazzling place, there will be no more death or mourning or crying or pain (Revelation 21:4). Every tear will be wiped away. Every sin and sorrow will be gone. Blind eyes will see and crippled legs will walk. It will be glorious, as well as beautiful. Can you imagine streets made of gold? And that is only the beginning.

Home. Finally, those of us with hearts surrendered to Jesus Christ will be in our forever home. Heaven is where each of us belongs.

Yes, one day the trumpet will sound and angels will sing. We will behold Him, our Lord and Savior. In fact, we will see Him *face-to-face*. Will you be present? Will your children and grandchildren stand by your side? Each individual must make that choice. What will you do to encourage, inform, and equip your loved ones to make the most important decision of their lives?

Your Heavenly Calling

We live in a fascinating but complex time. Never before have there been so many conveniences and technological gadgets. We have at our fingertips amazing opportunities. But it is also the most challenging of times. Our children and grandchildren live in a world abrasive to the ways of God. They are exposed to thoughts, actions, and comments that were completely unimaginable when we were young. God, in His stunning love and shrewd wisdom, has created us for such a time as this (Esther 4). Our destiny is to be His hands and feet to reach the hearts and lives of these loved ones. He wants us to minister to them on His behalf. Truly, this is a heavy calling.

Do not let the Enemy dishearten you. Immerse yourself in the following words of Isaiah, where he tells us we were sought from the far corners of the earth to be the Lord's chosen servants. Can you imagine? You were sought by the Lord. Also, take joy in the final verse. I am humbled and thrilled by these words where the Lord assures us that He will strengthen us and help us. He will uphold us in His righteous right hand.

Grandparents, you are held in the palm of His hand:

But you, Israel,
My servant, Jacob, whom I have chosen,
You descendants of Abraham my friend,
I took you from the ends of the earth,
From its farthest corners I called you.
I said, 'You are my servant';
I have chosen you and have not rejected you.

So do not fear, for I am with you;
Do not be dismayed, for I am your God.
I will strengthen you and help you;
I will uphold you with my righteous right hand.

Isaiah 41:8-10

I pray that The Seven Keys will empower you in your role as a grandparent. You can do this! I am excited at the potential of what the Lord can do through each of you. There are eighty million grandparents in the United States. Can you imagine what our country would be like if each of us picked up these keys and ran the race God has set before us? It is never too difficult, and it is never too late to be a grandparent making a difference. We are life changers for our children and grandchildren so that they can become *world changers*. Paul said it best in his first letter to the Corinthians: "What no eye has seen, what no ear has heard, and what no human mind has conceived—the things God has prepared for those who love him—these are the things God has revealed to us by his Spirit (1 Corinthians 2:9).

Run, Boy, Run!

In the last moments of the epic movie *Camelot*, King Arthur tells the story of Camelot to a young boy. Around the king are the remnants of the Knights of the Round Table. The end of an era is eminent. In the dim light of the dawning new day, the boy stares at his king, listening intently to his words. King Arthur stands and pulls the boy to his feet. There is fresh excitement in the king's eyes. He sees hope for the future in this young lad. All is not lost, the weary old king realizes. There is still a future for Camelot.

King Arthur says, "Go, young man! Go! Tell this story so that it won't be lost or forgotten."

At first, the lad hesitates. But after King Arthur gives him a piercing stare, the young boy starts to run, slowly at first. As he begins to run faster and faster, King Arthur throws back his head and yells, "Run, boy, run! Go! Tell the people so they won't forget. So the story will not be lost."[39]

Your Commission

Grandparents, the King of Glory bids you to run! Tell the greatest story that has ever been told. Tell your children and grandchildren about the everlasting love from our heavenly Father. Tell His story, and your story, so they will not be lost or forgotten. Share your words so the ring of truth resonates within the hearts of all you touch. Jesus is alive! He is real!

Run, grandparent, run! Grab your keys and pass a legacy of faith in Jesus Christ to your children and grandchildren. He is waiting for each one.

> I will sing of the Lord's great love forever;
> with my mouth I will make your
> faithfulness known through all generations.
> I will declare that your love stands firm forever,
> that you have established your faithfulness in heaven itself.
>
> PSALM 89:1-2

Study Questions

Chapter Ten: Run, Grandparent, Run

Pounding It Out

1. What is God's unbelievable destiny for grandparents?
    [To impact the hearts of our children and grandchildren
    by bringing them home to heaven] What is His goal?
    [For our families to spend eternity together]
2. Read Joshua 1:1–9. What does this passage tell us in
    verse 2? ["Get ready" to take the land the Lord gave
    you] What "land" does God want us to take? [Our
    children and grandchildren] In verses three, five, seven,
    and eight, what promises does the Lord make? In
    verse nine, the Lord commands us to be "strong and
    courageous." Why is there no reason to be afraid? [The
    Lord is with us everywhere we go]
3. How does the New Testament encourage grandparents?
    [Hebrews 12:1 says, "Therefore, since we are
    surrounded by such a great cloud of witnesses, let us
    throw off everything that hinders and the sin that so
    easily entangles. And let us run with perseverance
    the race marked out for us"] What hinders you from
    becoming a godly grandparent? What does the author
    of Hebrews tell us to do with these hindrances? [Throw
    them off] Remember, sin is anything we say, do, or
    think that separates us from the Lord. Is there any
    sin impeding your grandparent role? If so, what does

Hebrews command us to do? [Eliminate the sin that so easily entangles us]

Driving It Home

1. What are three reasons to become an intentional grandparent? [1) We are commanded in Matthew 28:19–20 to make disciples of all nations. Our families are our first mission field. 2) We are to do all we can to position our loved ones to live into God's purpose for their lives on this earth presently and in heaven eternally. 3) As spiritual beings, we will live forever. We want our loved ones to live in the presence of God rather than be forever separated from Him.]

2. Is heaven a real place? [Yes] Will you be there with your children and grandchildren by your side? How can you be certain you will all be there?

3. Is it too late to make a difference in the hearts and lives of your children and grandchildren? [No, it is never too late as long as there is breath in you and in your loved ones] During your daily prayer time, ask the Lord to reveal His way for you to become a life changer for your loved ones.

4. As the king of Camelot commands the lad to run and tell the story, so does the King of Glory bid you to run and tell His story. How can you share your story so that God's truth lives within the hearts of your children and grandchildren?

SPACEPETS:

AN ACRONYM FOR PERSONAL APPLICATION OF BIBLICAL TRUTHS

1. **Is there a SIN to confess?** Does this scripture passage make you realize you have a sin in your life that you need to tell the Lord?
2. **Is there a PROMISE to claim?** There are 7,000 promises in the Bible. As you read your Bible passage, search the text to see if there is a promise listed. Ask yourself if you have met all the conditions of the promise. Every promise has a premise.
3. **Is there an ATTITUDE to change?** Is there something you need to think about differently? Do you need to

work on a negative attitude, worry, guilt, fear, loneliness, bitterness, pride, apathy, or ego?

4. **Is there a COMMAND to obey?** Is there a command you need to obey, no matter how you feel?

5. **Is there an EXAMPLE to follow?** Are there positive examples to follow or negative examples to avoid?

6. **Is there a PRAYER to pray?** There are many prayers included in the text of the Bible. Often these prayers were uttered by one of God's extraordinary people. You can use their prayers knowing that you are speaking words of power and truth.

7. **Is there an ERROR to avoid?** Frequently we learn from our mistakes. It is better if we learn from the mistakes of others so that we save ourselves the pain or consequence of such/similar mistakes. As you study the Bible, what can you learn from the mistakes of those included in your scripture reading? [So, is there an error or faulty thinking listed in your Bible reading from which you can glean wisdom?]

8. **Is there a TRUTH to believe?** Throughout His Word, the Lord teaches us about various spiritual principles. These are truths for us to embrace so that we live the life God envisioned for us. [Often principles are included in scriptures that we simply need to believe.]

9. **Is there SOMETHING for which to praise God?** Scattered throughout Scripture are reminders of things for which to be thankful. Study your passage looking for reasons to praise the Lord.

Rick Warren. "SPACEPETS: Probe the Bible with These Questions." Pastor Rick's Daily Hope. PastorRick.com. 7 October 2014. http://pastorrick.com/devotional/english/spacepets-probe-the-biblewith-these-questions

APPENDIX B

CONVERSATION STARTERS FOR PURSUING HEALTHY RELATIONSHIPS

Whether you are pursuing a healthy relationship or catching up on the phone, here are some ideas for starting conversations:

1. What are three exciting things that have happened to you over the past week, month, or year?
2. What are three challenging matters that you have faced over the past week, month, or year?
3. Where do you see yourself in a year? Five years? Ten years?
4. What are your dreams? Expectations?
5. What are your frustrations? Fears? Anxieties?

Remember:

1. It is important that your adult child or grandchild feels you are listening to him.
2. If you are speaking in person, eye contact is important.
3. Make statements to encourage and affirm him or her.
4. Do not be too quick to offer solutions. Simply listen. Say, "I'm sure this is difficult."
5. Nod your head as you listen.
6. If your loved one asks for your opinion, give it. Otherwise, resist the urge to offer your perspective.
7. You are here to do all you can to help your loved one live fully into God's plan for his or her life. Offer to pray about any matter that your loved one shares with you.

Prayer for the Salvation
of a Grandchild

Dear Lord Jesus,

I lift up the soul of _____ to you. I pray, in the name of Jesus, that _____ would seek Your forgiveness for the sins in his life. May he trust fully in You for cleansing his heart so he can know You intimately, love You passionately, and serve You faithfully. I pray that _____ will live in such a way as to advance Your kingdom on this earth. Most of all, I pray that by Your grace, every one of my family members will arrive safely home in heaven.

In Jesus' name,
Amen

BLESSINGS RECORDED
IN SCRIPTURE

1. "The Lord bless you and keep you; the Lord make his face shine on you and be gracious to you; the Lord turn his face toward you and give you peace" (Numbers 6:24–26).
2. "May the grace of the Lord Jesus Christ, and the love of God, and the fellowship of the Holy Spirit be with you all" (2 Corinthians 13:14).
3. "Now may the God of peace, who through the blood of the eternal covenant brought back from the dead our Lord Jesus, that great Shepherd of the sheep, equip you with everything good for doing his will, and may he work in us what is pleasing to Him, through Jesus Christ, to whom be glory for ever and ever. Amen" (Hebrews 13:20–21).
4. "To Him who is able to keep you from stumbling and to present you before his glorious presence without fault

and with great joy—to the only God our Savior be glory, majesty, power and authority, through Jesus Christ our Lord, before all ages, now and forevermore! Amen" (Jude 24–25).

5. "May our Lord Jesus Christ himself and God our Father, who loved us and by his grace gave us eternal encouragement and good hope, encourage your hearts and strengthen you in every good deed and word" (2 Thessalonians 2:16–17).

6. "And the God of all grace, who called you to his eternal glory in Christ, after you have suffered a little while, will himself restore you and make you strong, firm and steadfast. To him be the power for ever and ever. Amen" (1 Peter 5:10–11).

7. "Now to him who is able to do immeasurably more than all we ask or imagine, according to his power that is at work within us, to him be glory in the church and in Christ Jesus throughout all generations, for ever and ever! Amen" (Ephesians 3:20–21).

8. "The grace of our Lord Jesus Christ be with you" (1 Thessalonians 5:28).

9. "Now to the King eternal, immortal, invisible, the only God, be honor and glory for ever and ever. Amen" (1 Timothy 1:17).

10. "The grace of the Lord Jesus be with God's people. Amen" (Revelation 22:21).

List of blessings taken from *The Hymnal for Worship and Celebration* (Waco, TX: Word Music, 1986), 613.

APPENDIX E

TIPS FOR SHARING THE GOSPEL WITH CHILDREN

1. Remember that Jesus welcomes children of any age to come to Him. See Matthew 19:14.
2. To prepare your own heart and sensitivity, pray before you share Christ with your loved one.
3. Discern a child's spiritual condition: Ready to respond? Struggling to understand? Resistant?
4. Open the Bible and use it to clearly share the gospel. Focus on a child's desire to trust Christ; avoid the tendency to prompt a child to pray a specific prayer, invite Christ into his or her "heart," or say the right words.
5. Encourage a child to express his or her faith (trust) in Jesus in their own words when they pray.
6. Use visuals from books to help communicate difficult words and concepts.

7. After a child responds to God's call, encourage him or her to tell other family members, friends, or a pastor.
8. Share the gospel with children individually, not in a group setting.
9. Go through the gospel presentation twice. Explain the gospel the first time, then when you review it, offer an opportunity to respond.
10. Do not manipulate a child to do what you want. Discern the heart attitude, then present the gospel to those you consider ready to trust Christ.

"Tips for Sharing Christ with Children" is a free resource provided by DiscipleLand.com. You can access it on the website. Click on "Good News for Kids: An Outline of Jesus' Message of Love and Forgiveness" under "Parent Tools." https://system.na3. netsuite.com/core/media/media.nl?id=7941&c=1155654&h=a-54288228afbc675bf4b&_xt=.pdf

ENDNOTES

1   "The Priorities, Challenges, and Trends in Youth Ministry,"
    Barna Group, April 2016 https://www.barna.com/
    researchthe-priorities-challenges-and-trends-in-youth-ministry/.

2   "America's Worldview," The Nehemiah Institute, October 3,
    2016 www.nehemiahinstitute.com/article.

3   Todd Phelps (sermon, Mosaic Church, Charlotte, NC,
    May 2009).

4   Joni Eareckson Tada, "Crown of Splendor," quoted in Doris
    Rikkers and Jeannette Taylor, *The Grandmother's Bible* (Grand
    Rapids: Zondervan, 2002), 867.

5   Quin M. Sherrer and Ruthanne Garlock, *Grandma, I Need Your
    Prayers* (Grand Rapids: Zondervan, 2002), 30.

6   Lillian Ann Penner, *Grandparenting with a Purpose*
    (Bloomington, Indiana: Crossbooks, 2010), xiv.

7   Cavin Harper quoted in Penner, ix.

8   Harper in Penner, ix.

9   Ruth Myers and Warren Myers, *31 Days of Praise* (Oregon:
    Multnomah, 1994), 100.

10 *The Book of Common Prayer and Administration of the
    Sacraments and Other Rites and Ceremonies of the Church
    Together with the Psalter or Psalms of David According to the*

Use of the Episcopal Church (New York, NY: Oxford University: 1979), pp. 362.

[11] Copies of this booklet available as a downloadable PDF on the author's website.

[12] Beth Moore, *Praying God's Word Day by Day* (Nashville: B&H Publishing Group, 2006), 79.

[13] Sherrer and Garlock, 214.

[14] "Pursue," *Roget's 21st Century Thesaurus*, Third Edition (New York: Random House, 2006), 669.

[15] "Integrity," *Merriam-Webster Unabridged Dictionary*. Online version. http://unabridged.merriam-webster.com/unabridged/integrity.

[16] Scott Turansky and Joanne Miller, *Say Goodbye to Whining, Complaining, and Bad Attitudes in You and Your Kids* (Colorado Springs: Waterbook Press, 2000), 13.

[17] Rob Rienow, *Never Too Late* (Grand Rapids: Kregel Publications, 2011). Summarized portions come from Chapter 4, 49-64; Chapter 5, 65-79; Chapter 7, 97–115. Permission to summarize the four steps was granted to the author by Dr. Rienow through personal communication.

[18] Rienow, 118–129. Permission to use the guidelines for establishing healthy relationships was granted to the author by Dr. Rienow through personal communication.

[19] Greg Vaughn, *Letters from Dad* (Nashville: Thomas Nelson, 2005), 13.

[20] Vaughn, 13.

[21] Vaughn, xi.

[22] Vaughn, xii.

[23] Vaughn, 166.

[24] Rienow, 139.

[25] Cavin Harper, "Unleashing the Power of the Spoken Blessing" (Workshop, Grace Church, Minneapolis, MN, May 2016).

[26] Cavin Harper, *Courageous Grandparenting* (Colorado Springs: Christian Grandparenting Network, 2013), 133.

27 Harper, "Unleashing the Power of the Spoken Blessing."
28 Harper, *Courageous Grandparenting*, 133.
29 Harper, *Courageous Grandparenting*, 133.
30 Harper, "Unleashing the Power of the Spoken Blessing."
31 A. Katherine Hankey, "I Love to Tell the Story," 1866. (Refrain by William G. Fischer, 1869), Public Domain.
32 Sherry Schumann, "The Testimony within You," (Sermon, Mount Carmel AME Church, Moncks Corner, SC, January 2016). Permission to use this statement granted to the author by Schumann through personal communication.
33 Lydia Harris, *Preparing My Heart for Grandparenting: For Grandparents at Any Stage of the Journey* (Chattanooga: AMG Publishers, 2010), 199.
34 Steven Green, "Find Us Faithful," YouTube video, 4:56, posted by Brianne Cipriano, April 20, 2010, http//www.youtube.com/watch?v=eERKnxzNzwg.
35 Cavin Harper, "The Blessing" (Courageous Grandparenting Conference, St. James Church, Charleston, SC, March, 2013).
36 Penner, 53.
37 Moore, 271.
38 Harper, "The Blessing."
39 *Camelot.* Joshua Logan, director, and Jack L. Warner, producer. Warner Brothers/Seven Arts, 1967.